I Am Who God Says I Am
Rejoicing in His Authority

Rev Kathryn L. Smith
Rejoicing in His Authority
Author of
There is Fire in the Blood
Meet Me on the Mountain, I Hear the Rocks Falling
Wilt Thou Be Made Whole

Earthly Stories with a Heavenly Meaning

I Am Who God Says I Am: Rejoicing in His Authority

Rev. Kathryn L. Smith

Author of There Is Fire In The Blood, Meet Me on the Mountain, I Hear the Rocks Falling and Wilt Thou Be Made Whole

Copyright © Kathryn L. Smith
February, 2018
Published By Parables
February, 2018

All Rights Reserved. No part of this book may be reproduced or utilized in any form or by any means, electronic or mechanical, including photocopying, recording, or by any information storage and retrieval system, without permission in writing from the author.

Unless otherwise specified Scripture quotations are taken from the authorized version of the King James Bible.

    ISBN 978-1-945698-47-7
    Printed in the United States of America

Readers should be aware that Internet Web sites offered as citations and/or sources for further information may have been changed or disappeared between the time this was written and when it is read.

I Am Who God Says I Am
Rejoicing in His Authority

Rev Kathryn L. Smith

Author of
There is Fire in the Blood
Meet Me on the Mountain, I Hear the Rocks Falling
Wilt Thou Be Made Whole

Earthly Stories with a Heavenly Meaning

KATHRYN L. SMITH

Table of Contents

13	Identity
23	Usurped Authority
33	Real Authority
43	Bridging Eternity
55	Binding the Strong Man
63	Dead Lions
75	In Christ
85	Dressed for Success
93	Use the Name
107	What Did You Say
117	Sharing the Victory
125	Walking by Faith
135	Not by Sight
147	Fear No Devil
155	Salt & Light
163	Resurrection Power
173	Who Do You Say You Are
181	Works Cited
182	Author Page

Acknowledgements

It is with deepest reverence that I dedicate this book to Rev. Timothy A. Naylor a man worthy of double honor, who is both my Pastor and my friend. He has always respected the call of God on my life and has given me great liberty, prayerful support and guidance. He has faithfully ministered the Word that fed my spirit, and he has been an example of both integrity and in carrying the anointing.

I deeply appreciate all those who made me the woman of faith, the minister, and the author that I am. I want to especially thank Pastor Rick Naylor, who taught me what it meant to be called and how to minister. He taught me faith, and to trust in the indisputable Word of God. These pastors and other men of faith have invested in my spiritual growth and served as shepherds to my soul. I also want to express my gratitude to all the men and women whose ministries and books have shaped my faith; some of those names have faded over time, but their truths have become ingrained within my spirit; to all those who taught me and nurtured me, but were not specifically cited in this book—thank you.

I want to thank the people who so kindly and consistently encouraged me, and those who have purchased and read my books. I wish to extend special gratitude to Donna Naylor who was the first to read each of my books and who graciously did some editing. She helped me with grammar and punctuation, while always honoring the message within the text.

Thank you to my dear husband, Buzz who patiently endured countless hours alone while I ministered or wrote. I deeply love and appreciate the man of God that he is and the constant love that he shows me.

Mostly, I want to thank the Lord Jesus Christ who loved me when I was unlovely, saved me when I was lost, called me when I was nothing and anointed me to do His work. I pray that He will be glorified and lifted high in all I have attempted for Him.

Matthew 3:17 (KJV) *17 And lo a voice from heaven, saying, This is my beloved Son, in whom I am well pleased.*

Identity

Identity is who we really are, not just the perceptions of those around us. It is not that important what other people think, or who others think we are. In contrast, it really matters who we believe we are. For too long, we have allowed men to shape our ideas and self-image. They try to determine the measure of our worth and our role in this world. What really matters is who God says we are. We are who we are based not on society's opinion or even our own, but based upon what God has said about us. He says we are His beloved children. God says we are His treasure, chosen and blessed beyond our comprehension. He says we have dominion and authority by inheritance. God the Father says we have the right to use the Name of Jesus to overcome all the world throws our way.

When the devil or the world comes and says, "Just who do you think you are?" I have an answer. I am blessed and highly favored. I am saved, I am anointed and I am called, because God says I am; so are you. When the great I AM says I am something it is true.

I didn't always know that. I wasn't what you would call a planned pregnancy. My mother was told, after a very difficult breach birth, that there would be no more children.

But by her six week checkup, she was pregnant with me. Maybe I wasn't planned and maybe I wasn't even wanted but I was destined to be something that God wanted me to be. I am who I am because He says I am. God had a plan and a purpose in my being here. I don't believe there is any life that is not God breathed. God doesn't make mistakes and for what it is worth, you and I are here for a purpose.

David said that God was there when we were conceived and formed. **Psalm 139:13-16 (KJV)** *13 For thou hast possessed my reins: thou hast covered me in my mother's womb. 14 I will praise thee; for I am fearfully and wonderfully made: marvellous are thy works; and that my soul knoweth right well. 15 My substance was not hid from thee, when I was made in secret, and curiously wrought in the lowest parts of the earth. 16 Thine eyes did see my substance, yet being unperfect; and in thy book all my members were written, which in continuance were fashioned, when as yet there was none of them.* That doesn't sound like a mistake, but rather a design.

God spoke in similar fashion to Jeremiah, when He called him to serve as a prophet. **Jeremiah 1:4-10 (KJV)** *4 Then the word of the LORD came unto me, saying, 5 Before I formed thee in the belly I knew thee; and before thou camest forth out of the womb I sanctified thee, and I ordained thee a prophet unto the nations. 6 Then said I, Ah, Lord GOD! behold, I cannot speak: for I am a child. 7 But the LORD said unto me, Say not, I am a child: for thou shalt go to all that I shall send thee, and whatsoever I command thee thou shalt speak. 8 Be not afraid of their faces: for I am with thee to deliver thee, saith the LORD. 9 Then the LORD put forth his hand, and touched my mouth. And the LORD said unto me, Behold, I have put my words in thy mouth. 10 See, I have this day set thee over the nations and over the kingdoms, to root* out, and to pull down, and to destroy, and to throw down, to build, and to plant.* God ordained all of that when Jeremiah thought he was nothing. He can work with us too.

Since God is so involved with us even before we are born, He must love us and highly value us. **Song of Songs 6:3 (KJV)** *3 I am my beloved's, and my beloved is mine...* Look what it says about us belonging to God in the Old Testament. **Deuteronomy 32: 9 (KJV).** *9 For the LORD'S portion is his people; Jacob is the lot of his inheritance.* While this speaks of Israel in the Old Testament, all who will respond to His invitation, become part of God's chosen people, the bride of Christ, and His inheritance in the New Testament. He loves us with an everlasting, sin forgiving, past forgetting, life changing love.

Remember that even when Jesus walked the earth some received Him for who He really was, and others judged and condemned Him. It never moved Him from His Father's love or His divine purpose. You might not think you are much but Jesus thinks you are worth dying for. He could have stayed in heaven, He could have walked away when condemned to die on the cross but instead He chose to die that you would have eternal life. He made you a member of God's family. He called you His own. No matter what the world thinks, God has chosen to pour out His love on you.

Mark 8:27-29 (KJV) *27 And Jesus went out, and his disciples, into the towns of Caesarea Philippi: and by the way he asked his disciples, saying unto them, Whom do men say that I am? 28 And they answered, John the Baptist: but some say, Elias; and others, One of the prophets.* Jesus knew the world had a mixture of opinions about Him. He was not concerned with public sentiment. It did matter what His followers thought. If they believed in who He really was, and still is, He could use that to change who they believed they were. *29 And he saith unto them, But whom say ye that I am? And Peter answereth and saith unto him, Thou art the Christ.*

God had already declared who Jesus was, but it still came as a revelation to Peter. God would establish His Church on the revelation that Jesus was the very Son of God; He was the Messiah—the Anointed One. Twice God spoke those words into the atmosphere. First, God spoke at the Lord's baptism. **Matthew 3:16-17 (KJV)** *16 And Jesus, when he was baptized, went up straightway out of the water: and, lo, the heavens were opened unto him, and he saw the Spirit of God descending like a dove, and lighting upon him: 17 And lo a voice from heaven, saying, This is my beloved Son, in whom I am well pleased.* [My dad said that about me once not long before he died and I will always cherish it.] God spoke those words again on the Mountain of Transfiguration. **Matthew 17:5 (KJV)** *5 While he yet spake, behold, a bright cloud overshadowed them: and behold a voice out of the cloud, which said, This is my beloved Son, in whom I am well pleased; hear ye him.* Those words from heaven sustained the believers and gave them confidence that the Son of God had come and that they were united to Him.

We are God's own chosen people. We did not earn that, we might not deserve it, but it is our positon in Christ. **Hebrews 4:16 (KJV)** *16 Let us therefore come boldly unto the throne of grace, that we may obtain mercy, and find grace to help in time of need.* "You can come boldly because you come to God by the blood of Jesus Christ and not by how you have lived your life. So whenever you come into God's presence, you don't have to be afraid your sins will be exposed because the blood of Jesus has removed every one of them; He sees only the blood of His Son, which has been shed for your total forgiveness and acceptance." (Prince 9/28/17) When we came to God, asking Him to save us, He did. He poured out great mercy and divine grace. Mercy means we don't get punished as we should and grace means He gave us what we had no way of obtaining on our own. "Grace means you get the good things that you don't deserve, such as health, protection, anointing, favor, and good success and a life more abundant." (Prince 9/28/17) More than any of those things, God gave you a new identity. You became His. When God saved you, you were born again—grafted into His family.

Some might call me a teacher, a preacher or an author. To some I am a mother, a sister, a friend. Those are all roles I fill but they do not define me. I am who I am because of who He is in me. I am the Lord's beloved. I am saved and filled with His precious Spirit. I am whatever He says I am and I can do whatever He says I can do. And so can you! **Isaiah 61:1-3 (KJV)** *1 The Spirit of the Lord GOD is upon me; because the LORD hath anointed me to preach good tidings unto the meek; he hath sent me to bind up the brokenhearted, to proclaim liberty to the captives, and the opening of the prison to them that are bound; 2 To proclaim the acceptable year of the LORD, and the day of vengeance of our God; to comfort all that mourn; 3 To appoint unto them that mourn in Zion, to give unto them beauty for ashes, the oil of joy for mourning, the garment of praise for the spirit of heaviness; that they might be called trees of righteousness, the planting of the LORD, that he might be glorified.* That is who Jesus was.

He was the truest servant of God. Jesus walked in the office of prophet and priest and king. He served well in each capacity, based on what the Father had spoken over

Him and the power of the Holy Spirit within and upon Him. We work the same way. He was sent to preach hope and salvation. He was sent to heal and to comfort. Jesus was sent to mend what was broken within men and to tell them they could be saved. He proclaimed liberty to those in bondage and hope to those who felt distress. Jesus came to release those in bondage to sin and to bring them into joyous freedom. Since we are one with Him, then that is also who we are through the blood that He shed. We are the called, the sent, the anointed, and we are commissioned to do His work. We are more than enough for whatever He wants us to do. There is nothing that can stop us, because we are His.

Jesus did not leave believers alone on the earth. He sent to us another member of the Trinity, His Holy Spirit. **John 14:16-17 (KJV)** *16 And I will pray the Father, and he shall give you another Comforter, that he may abide with you forever; 17 Even the Spirit of truth; whom the world cannot receive, because it seeth him not, neither knoweth him: but ye know him; for he dwelleth with you, and shall be in you.* Jesus said that the Comforter had been with them, and just like the Old Testament prophets, they had done miracles by the Spirit falling on them, but now that Spirit would be in them. He continued teaching about the role of the Holy Spirit in our lives. **John 16:7-14 (YLT)** *7But I tell you the truth; it is better for you that I go away, for if I may not go away, the Comforter will not come unto you, and if I go on, I will send Him unto you... 12 I have yet many things to say to you, but ye are not able to bear them now; 13 and when He may come—the Spirit of truth—He will guide you to all the truth, for He will not speak from Himself, but as many things as He will hear He will speak, and the coming things He will tell you; 14 He will glorify me, because of mine He will take, and will tell to you.* It was the job of the Holy Spirit to indwell believers and to enable us to represent the Lord on earth.

Just before Jesus ascended to heaven He told the disciples to wait for the Holy Spirit to empower them. **Acts 1:8 (KJV)** *8 But ye shall receive power, after that the Holy Ghost is come upon you: and ye shall be witnesses unto me both in Jerusalem, and in all Judaea, and in Samaria, and unto the uttermost part of the earth.* Jesus spoke to the disciples and that word still speaks to us as believers. "He did not say, you will do witnessing, but you shall be witnesses. In other words, your very person will be a witness to Him!" (Prince 10/21/17) One of the descriptions of the believer is that we have become a testimony to His goodness and His presence and our very lives proclaim Jesus as Lord. We do not have to do this alone for we have His power, His ability resident within us to make us effective witness. He said we are His witnesses so we are. We don't have anything to prove; we are just living out the decree of the All Powerful Living God.

Look what the Apostle Paul wrote about us. **Romans 8:31-39 (KJV)** *31 What shall we then say to these things? If God be for us, who can be against us? 32 He that spared not his own Son, but delivered him up for us all, how shall he not with him also freely give us all things? 33 Who shall lay anything to the charge of God's elect? It is God that justifieth. 34 Who is he that condemneth? It is Christ that died, yea rather, that is risen again, who is even at the right hand of God, who also maketh intercession for us. 35 Who shall separate us from the love of Christ? shall tribulation, or distress, or persecution, or famine, or nakedness, or peril, or sword? 36 As it is written, For thy sake we are killed all the day long; we are accounted as sheep for the slaughter. 37 Nay, in all these things we are more than conquerors through* *him that loved us. 38 For I am persuaded, that neither death, nor life, nor angels, nor principalities, nor powers, nor things present, nor things to come, 39 Nor height, nor depth, nor any other creature, shall be able to separate us from the love of God, which is in Christ Jesus our Lord.* It was true of the early church and it still applies to every born again believer. We are more than conquerors, not because of our own ability or goodness, but because we have entered into perfect union with Him. He said it, so we know it is true.

More than anything else, we are loved. God cares about us. We are constantly in His heart and on His mind. **Psalm 139:17-18 (KJV)** *17 How precious also are thy thoughts unto me, O God! how great is the sum of them! 18 If I should count them, they are more in number than the sand: when I awake, I am still with thee.* In a world where most people feel desperately lonely and inadequate, we are loved by God and that love defines us.

I Am Who God Says I Am

Genesis 1:27-28 *(KJV) 27 So God created man in his own image, in the image of God created he him; male and female created he them. 28 And God blessed them, and God said unto them, Be fruitful, and multiply, and replenish the earth, and subdue it: and have dominion over the fish of the sea, and over the fowl of the air, and over every living thing that moveth upon the earth.*

Usurped Authority

There is a vast difference between authority that is delegated and authority that has been stolen. When God created Adam, He gave him absolute authority, total dominion over planet earth and all that would ever be born here. God intended for man to rule over His creation. For a time that is exactly what happened. But eventually, the enemy of God came and usurped that authority by deception. That old thief, the devil, came to Adam intending to steal that authority. His goal was to kill mankind and destroy all of creation. [John 10:10]

Genesis 1:27-28 (KJV) *27 So God created man in his own image, in the image of God created he him; male and female created he them. 28 And God blessed them, and God said unto them, Be fruitful, and multiply, and replenish the earth, and subdue it: and have dominion over the fish of the sea, and over the fowl of the air, and over every living thing that moveth upon the earth.* Adam held the title deed to this planet and all that it contained. He was the undisputed ruler of the earth as long as he walked in unity with the Creator. God had established a new order of beings that were like the Godhead. Humans were higher than the order of angels. They possessed intelligence and free will. They were not all knowing and they were inexperienced, but they were God-men. For a season, mankind was immortal, possessing an inheritance in the earth.

"The fallen displaced Lucifer was in Eden observing God as He made man. He watched and pondered deeply as the Creator formed man from a small bit of dust, but the words he heard are what excited him." (Trombley p. 62) Man had dominion. Man ruled here. If the devil could get man to disobey, he could take that place of lordship. Satan always wanted to be like God, to be in charge, to be worshiped and he thought that man and earth were his chance. Satan determined to steal by deception what was given to man.

I like the way Charles Trombley described it almost as if he were hearing the devil speak. "I'll have a twofold objective, he pondered. If there's some way I can persuade him to eat of that tree, he would release that authority to me, and being a legal transaction, bound by God's absolute honesty, I can pick it up. Once I break his dependence on God and get him to act on his own, he'll be doing the same thing I did and he'll be joined to me. After all, I too, had such authority and I lost it when I acted independently of God and developed my own will. One thing is certain, this man is created in His image, so God can't reclaim it without another exactly like him challenging me, and he's one of a kind!" (Trombley p. 63) After the fall, God could not go back to the clay and form another man. Everything on earth was tainted by Adam's rebellion.

For a while, Adam and Eve walked with God and enjoyed the freedom of the garden. Slowly, that evil one came, not to man, who had the full legal authority, but to his wife. She was the most precious thing on earth to Adam, a gift from the Creator and very bone of his bone. Adam loved her dearly. So she became the focus of Satan's attack.

Remember the devil didn't come as some ugly, slithering snake. He was the fallen Lucifer, son of the morning. He came in beauty and shining with light and he was subtle in his ways. His plan was to get her to doubt just a little, to think that God may have withheld something from her. He took his time. Eve had never encountered deception; she had no frame of reference for lies. They had perfect trust because their Creator had always been truthful and kind. Adam and Eve lived in a perfect world. There was no sin, no danger. They did not know they should be wary of this creature. Eve didn't have the scripture that warns us to guard our hearts. All she knew was good and she was totally open to all that she saw and heard.

Her innocence made Eve an easy mark for the devil. I believe the devil came to her repeatedly over a period of time. He was patient. He built a rapport with her; he became a companion that spoke to her. He made observations and shared some truths at first and then he inserted tiny lies. Day by day, the devil sowed little seeds of doubt, curiosity and rebellion into Eve's fertile heart.

Eventually, he spoke what was really the core of his deception. **Genesis 3:1-8 (KJV)** *1 Now the serpent was more subtil than any beast of the field which the LORD God had made. And he said unto the woman, Yea, hath God said, Ye shall not eat of every tree of the garden?* That serpent spoke to her like he does to all of mankind. God didn't really say that, did He? Well, God didn't really mean it. God might not be telling you the whole story; He is withholding something from you. He came with a distortion, you can't eat at all… *2 And the woman said unto the serpent, We may eat of the fruit of the trees of the garden: 3 But of the fruit of the tree which is in the midst of the garden, God hath said, Ye shall not* *eat of it, neither shall ye touch it, lest ye die.* He sees some ray of hope, for she added to the command of God. There was nothing wrong with touching the tree. It violated no command. If she touched it and nothing happened, he could distort the command even more. A little doubt goes a long way. He called God a liar. Adam and Eve have no reference for death. There in the garden, nothing aged or decayed; death was just a meaningless word. *4 And the serpent said unto the woman, Ye shall not surely die: 5 For God doth know that in the day ye eat thereof, then your eyes shall be opened, and ye shall be as gods, knowing good and evil.* Don't you want to be more like God? God is withholding this area of knowledge to keep you in submission. The great lie, God is not perfect love and truth. God is not always good. You are missing out on something. You can be wise. *6 And when the woman saw that the tree was good for food, and that it was pleasant to the eyes, and a tree to be desired to make one wise, she took of the fruit thereof, and did eat, and gave also unto her husband with her; and he did eat.*

I always kind of hoped that Adam was off tending to some crops but unfortunately, he was right there letting the devil tempt his wife. He could have stopped all of this with one word, but he didn't speak up when the devil was tempting her. He did not knock the fruit from her hand. He did not say wait a minute devil you don't have any right to be here, get out. He did not use his God given authority. He did not draw Eve into his arms and whisper words of wisdom to her. No, he just let it happen, and then he joined her in sin.

Eve fell by deception, but Adam openly chose to be with her over God. Adam who had dominion threw it away. *7 And the eyes of them both were opened, and they knew that they were naked; and they sewed fig leaves together, and made themselves aprons.* When Adam sinned, he realized the glory had vanished; the flame of God within him had gone out. He no longer looked like God; Adam was indeed naked. His heart and his flesh no longer reflected God on the earth. *8 And they heard the voice of the LORD God walking in the garden in the cool of the day: and Adam and his wife hid themselves from the presence of the LORD God amongst the trees of the garden.* Their sin made them recoil from the One who had loved them and fellowshipped with them. They ran away from the One they had always run to. Sin had separated them from their Creator. It is the same seed of sin that rips man away from God today. Sin always creates a barrier for fellowship.

There is no record that Adam and Eve tried to repent. When confronted with their rebellion they chose to point the finger at another. They had already learned to lie and to blame rather than to take responsibility for their actions. We can clearly see how that tendency has grown to maturity in our world. **Genesis 3:12-13 (KJV)** *12 And the man said, The woman whom thou gavest to be with me, she gave me of the tree, and I did eat.* It almost sounds like Adam was putting the fault on God for giving him a wife. *13 And the LORD God said unto the woman, What is this that thou hast done? And the woman said, The serpent beguiled me, and I did eat.* It was Eve's fault. To some extent maybe it was, but legally it was not. And we can't even blame the devil. Adam was in charge. If he did not partake of that fruit, he could have interceded for Eve and maybe there would still be hope for humanity. He could have chosen God over Eve and we would have had a chance. Instead he rebelled; he willingly yielded to the devil and mankind was lost. Adam chose to be independent of God and from that moment forward, mankind would be separated from Him. Spiritual death would come to all.

Romans 6:23 (KJV) *23 For the wages of sin is death; but the gift of God is eternal life through Jesus Christ our Lord.* "The moment Adam sinned, he died spiritually, but he didn't die physically for years. Spiritual death came first, finally manifesting itself through the physical death. Genesis 5:5 tells us he was 930 years old when death finally took him. The moment spiritual death overtook him; he was mortal, subject to death, or death-doomed. All humanity sprang from Adam and was identified in his spiritual death. Death passed upon all men by inheritance. **Romans 5: 21 (KJV)** *21 That as sin hath reigned unto death, [even so might grace reign through righteousness unto eternal life by Jesus Christ our Lord].* Spiritual death, the nature of Satan, like a hideous dictator, seized the control, sovereignty and dominion over creation." (Trombley p. 74) Adam was demoted spiritually, his life mutated into death. He became another type of being, a fallen man; he became mortal.

Every person who would ever take a breath was within Adam so when he fell, we fell. And now he had obeyed Satan, so he is servant to Satan. **Romans 6:16 (KJV)** *16 Know ye not, that to whom ye yield yourselves servants to obey, his servants ye are to whom ye obey; whether of sin unto death, or of obedience unto righteousness?* Adam had disconnected from the source of life. Now Adam is connected to, joined to, and covenanted with the enemy of God. Now the whole of mankind is doomed. The deed to planet earth changed hands. The devil is in control here and he rules with a fist of iron. Evil permeated the whole of creation. Satan became the god of this world by default. Adam's lordship was over; he became the slave of sin and death. If only he had stopped Eve. "Because he failed to exercise his dominion over all God's works, including this serpent before him, he defaulted and deliberately allowed himself to come under Satan's dominion." (Trombley p. 70)

The whole of planet earth was under Adam's authority and the tainted clay belonged to the devil. God would not create another as He had created Adam. The devil thought he had a perfect plan. But there would be a second Adam; another God-man would come many generations later. This one would be born to a virgin and His name was Jesus.

That old serpent, the devil, tempted Eve with the lust of the eyes, the lust of the flesh and the pride of life. Those were the same three areas of temptation we see recorded when Jesus faced him in the wilderness. But Jesus resisted him. We know that the devil offered all the kingdoms of the world to Jesus if he would bow down. [Luke 4:1-13] Jesus refused, but He never said that Satan lied. He did have that authority; it was turned over to him in the garden and he could give it to anyone he wanted. He is still holding strong to that deed. "Sin is our birthright as human beings. We are born into it. However, righteousness is our birthright as Christians. We are born into it through the new birth and no longer have an inheritance of sin." (Dollar p.17) You are the righteousness of God because God said so. You were bound by sin but not any longer. You are free and made clean because Jesus took your place.

There was still hope for mankind. **John 10:10 (KJV)** *10 The thief cometh not, but for to steal, and to kill, and to destroy: I am come that they might have life, and that they might have it more abundantly.* God had a plan to redeem us even before we needed it. He sent His very own Son Jesus, to come and rescue us. He willingly took our place, and covered the whole of sin's debt. Jesus paid in full for our redemption and offered us salvation for the taking.

"Jesus systematically stripped the defeated Satan before the host of heaven, and earth and hell. He was not allowed to retain even the weakest aspect of authority, or recognition, lest he make a second claim." (Trombley p.104) At the cross, man was given a way out of Satan's dominion. After the cross, men could finally come out from under that bondage. The whole human race did not partake of redemption, but it was available to all. The earth itself was not affected, but individuals could leave bondage behind and find real life through Jesus.

Ephesians 2:1-8 (KJV) *1 And you hath he quickened, who were dead in trespasses and sins; 2 Wherein in time past ye walked according to the course of this world, according to the prince of the power of the air, the spirit that now worketh in the children of disobedience: 3 Among whom also we all had our conversation in times past in the lusts of our flesh, fulfilling the desires of the flesh and of the mind; and were by nature the children of wrath, even as others. 4 But God, who is rich in mercy, for his great love wherewith he loved us, 5 Even when we were dead in sins, hath quickened us together with Christ, (by grace ye are saved;) 6 And hath raised us up together, and made us sit together in heavenly places in Christ Jesus: 7 That in the ages to come he might shew the exceeding riches of his grace in his kindness toward us through Christ Jesus. 8 For by grace are ye saved through faith; and that not of yourselves: it is the gift of God:*

There is an old Bob Dylan Song called Gotta Serve Somebody. "It may be the devil or it may be the Lord but you're gonna have to serve somebody." Until you found Christ, you were automatically the servant of the devil. You were forced to live in his fallen world. You were made to live under bondage to sin and sickness and death. Now you have a choice.

Once you are saved, you are born into a new kingdom and become a new species. You become like Adam and Eve before the fall. **II Corinthians 5:17-18 (KJV)** *17 Therefore if any man be in Christ, he is a new creature: old things are passed away; behold, all things are become new. 18 And all things are of God, who hath reconciled us to himself by Jesus Christ, and hath given to us the ministry of reconciliation;* "Everything Satan took away from Adam, Jesus took back. Everything he put in Adam, Jesus took out. Everything he put on him, Jesus took off. Satan's works were completely undone; they were rendered powerless and ineffective." (Trombley p. 105) God brought full redemption through the blood of Jesus.

Through the sacrifice of Jesus, the results of the fall are able to be reversed. "He conquered and is now the Lord of both heaven and earth. He now holds the delegated authority Adam lost. The universe is back in control of the heavenlies. Single-handedly He vanquished sin and death. Jesus is the Lord of Hosts." (Trombley p. 103) Once you believe that the Lord died in your place, death has no hold on you. Once you know that sin was paid for, you are no longer a slave to sin. Everything the devil took by deception has been restored. His hold has been broken and the reborn of mankind are free to walk in a place of authority in the earth again. The devil held his usurped authority for generations, but he is no longer the god of this world. We have given allegiance to a Greater One. Jesus is Lord and He has set the captives free.

Matthew 28:18 (KJV) *18 And Jesus came and spake unto them, saying, All power is given unto me in heaven and in earth. 19 Go ye therefore,*

Real Authority

Many Christians do not know that we have the right and the commission to stand against every worldly attack and withstand every enemy with the same power and authority that Jesus demonstrated. When we were born again, we were given the right to use the name of Jesus to enforce His victory. We became Christ's ambassadors. **Ephesians 6:10 (KJV)** *10 Finally, my brethren, be strong in the Lord, and in the power of his might.* That is delegated authority. We are given the power to stand in His might, His position. None of us stands in our own strength or ability. We are able to do whatever is necessary because we are one with the Lord.

When I say that we have authority, I mean that we are included in the death and resurrection of Jesus and He has given us the right and responsibility to enforce His victory. It is not dependent upon our education, our church membership or any title we might hold. We are in a position of authority because we are saved. We do not possess some special knowledge or ability of our own. As believers, we are recipients of what Jesus has already done for us. We have dominion by position. Jesus defeated the devil and sin and death and He gave us a position in Him that grants us access to the spoils of war. **Matthew 28:18 (NIV)** *18 Then Jesus came to them and said, "All authority in heaven and on earth* *has been given to me.* God the Father conferred that power or authority on Christ and then He delegated it to us. **Matthew 28:18-20 (KJV)** *18 And Jesus came and spake unto them, saying, All power is given unto me in heaven and in earth. 19 Go ye therefore, and teach all nations, baptizing them in the name of the Father, and of the Son, and of the Holy Ghost: 20 Teaching them to observe all things whatsoever I have commanded you: and, lo, I am with you alway, even unto the end of the world. Amen.*

As Christians, we are His ambassadors on the earth. Jesus defeated the devil. He told us that we represent Him and He also promised that we would never stand and face the enemy alone. That means we present Him and His victory through our daily lives. We show the world the victorious One by using His authority.

Jesus delegated authority to the twelve disciples, then to the seventy and finally to all believers. He took His own power and dominion and passed it on to those who would continue His work. **Luke 9:1-2 (KJV)** *1 Then he called his twelve disciples together, and gave them power and authority over all devils, and to cure diseases. 2 And he sent them to preach the kingdom of God, and to heal the sick.*

In like manner, He sent out a larger group with similar directions and delegated authority. **Luke 10:1 (KJV)** *1 After these things the Lord appointed other seventy also, and sent them two and two before his face into every city and place, whither he himself would come.* **Luke 10:17-20 (KJV)** *17 And the seventy returned again with joy, saying, Lord, even the devils are subject unto us through thy name. 18 And he said unto them, I beheld Satan as lightning fall from heaven. 19 Behold, I give unto you power to tread on* *serpents and scorpions, and over all the power of the enemy: and nothing shall by any means hurt you. 20 Notwithstanding in this rejoice not, that the spirits are subject unto you; but rather rejoice, because your names are written in heaven.* In verse 19 we see two words translated as power. First, it says I give you power to tread on serpents and scorpions. That word for power is ***exousia*** which means authority and jurisdiction, the right to make commands and demands is included in the word. The second word translated power is ***dunamis*** which means ability, strength and might. So Jesus told them you have the right to assume legal and lawful control over all the ability and strength of the devil. That is a very powerful statement. Jesus, the Son of God, came and used His confidence in the Father, which is the definition of faith, and ruled over the devil. Then He told them to go and use His name to do the same. He did not limit or restrict His followers, but trusted them with amazing power and authority. You were given authority because you were included in that commission.

There is incredible power available to Christians. We have a God given authority and when we know it, it will work for us. General Wainwright suffered greatly in a Manchurian concentration camp during World War II. "There were several Japanese guards who tormented him daily. He was subjected to unforgettable atrocities. Half-starved, without proper nutrition, he soon became a skeleton, a broken, helpless, crushed, abused, trapped shadow of the powerful commander he once was." When a member of his own staff came into the camp and announced that Japan had unconditionally surrendered, his entire countenance changed. "Later when his tormentors, apparently unaware of what had happened, returned to ridicule and mock him, he barked, "I'm in command here now! And you will obey my orders. Japan has been soundly defeated and all of your authority over me has been cancelled." Shocked, almost to the point of disbelief, the guards knew that he was informed of their defeat. They immediately submitted." (Trombley p. 19-20) The only difference at the end of the day was in what the General believed and what his former captors, who were now prisoners, believed. He no longer stood there alone but his words were backed by the whole of the Allied Forces. He was using the authority given to him. He was no stronger physically than he was yesterday, but now he knew he was in command. My brothers and sisters in Christ, look at that as a picture of us. We were held in bondage by sin and the devil abused us at will, but then One stronger came in and conquered him. When Jesus defeated the devil, and paid in full for sin and death, we were made free. We were given our freedom and the right to rule over our captor.

Our victor was Jesus and He delegated the power that He won to those who represent Him. When you recognize the fact that He is the head of the church and we as the church are authorized to exercise His victory, you see yourself standing in a secured place. It is not because you feel powerful or think you are something, it is not anything you have said or done. It is because God said so. God's word put you in the position of authority.

Look at what the Apostle Paul wrote as his continual desire for the believers. **Ephesians 1:17-23 (KJV)** *17 That the God of our Lord Jesus Christ, the Father of glory, may give unto you the spirit of wisdom and revelation in the knowledge of him: 18 The eyes of your understanding being enlightened; that ye may know what is the hope of his calling, and what the riches of the glory of his inheritance in the saints,19 And what is the exceeding greatness of his power to us-ward who believe, according to the working* *of his mighty power,20 Which he wrought in Christ, when he raised him from the dead, and set him at his own right hand in the heavenly places ,21 Far above all principality, and power, and might, and dominion, and every name that is named, not only in this world, but also in that which is to come: 22 And hath put all things under his feet, and gave him to be the head over all things to the church, 23 Which is his body, the fulness of him that filleth all in all.* Jesus soundly defeated the devil and then sat down in the place of authority in heaven and told you that you share His throne and His victory. It is not something you have to earn or strive for. It is yours by inheritance; it is your legal right as a believer.

Colossians 2:15 (KJV) *15 And having spoiled principalities and powers, he made a shew of them openly, triumphing over them in it* [the cross]. There is no longer any enemy that is not defeated. He put all things under His feet, just like every king that took captive a defeated enemy. Jesus stood over the defeated one with His foot on the enemy's throat. His actions show the complete domination of the one He defeated. Victory over the devil and all that was his has already been accomplished and you are set in the body as a conqueror. You have the right to use His name. Your relationship with Christ empowers you to enforce His victory. "Notice that not only is Christ seated at the right hand of the Father, above all powers in Satan's realm, but we're there too, because God *has raised us up together.* Not only have we been made to sit, but notice where we are sitting: *far above all principality, and power, and might and dominion."* (Hagin p. 27)

Ephesians 2:4-7 (KJV) *4 But God, who is rich in mercy, for his great love wherewith he loved us, 5 Even when we were dead in sins, hath quickened us together with*

Christ, He made us alive, resurrected us in Jesus. *(by grace ye are saved;) 6 And hath raised us up together, and made us sit together in heavenly places in Christ Jesus: 7 That in the ages to come he might shew the exceeding riches of his grace in his kindness toward us through Christ Jesus.* God gave us life in Jesus and that was not a defeated and broken life. It is a victorious life. **I Corinthians 15:21-27 (KJV)** *21 For since by man came death, by man came also the resurrection of the dead. 22 For as in Adam all die, even so in Christ shall all be made alive. 23 But every man in his own order: Christ the firstfruits; afterward they that are Christ's at his coming. 24 Then cometh the end, when he shall have delivered up the kingdom to God, even the Father; when he shall have put down all rule and all authority and power. 25 For he must reign, till he hath put all enemies under his feet. 26 The last enemy that shall be destroyed is death. 27 For he hath put all things under his feet...* Jesus established His victory and put all things under His feet. The feet are in the body. We who are the body of Christ have the enemy under our feet.

I wanted to add something here that I never noticed before. When looking at His overall victory I was studying in the book of Isaiah and found this. **Isaiah 53:12 (KJV)** *12 Therefore will I divide him a portion with the great, and he shall divide the spoil with the strong; because he hath poured out his soul unto death: and he was numbered with the transgressors; and he bare the sin of many, and made intercession for the transgressors.* In light of the victory and the spoils of war, it sounds to me like we share in the bounty of what He won. **Isaiah 53:12 (NASB)** *12 Therefore, I will allot Him a portion with the great, And He will divide the booty with the strong...* **Isaiah 53:12 (GW)** *12 So I will give him a share among the mighty, and he will divide the prize with the strong...* If I am seeing that right, we were made strong where we had been weak because of sin. Since we are now in Christ, we share in His victory and part of the spoils go to us. We get what He won. We know that He took back total dominion of all Adam lost. Mankind was released from the hold of sin and death. We also know that sickness, poverty and oppression were a direct result of the fall. If Jesus won back all Adam lost, then gave it to us, we have victory over all of the effects of the fall. We get back all that was taken from mankind. We are numbered among the strong and victorious ones who now possess the fullness of what was gained by the Lord's death. We have the victory. We have salvation. As believers, we already own healing and deliverance. We were included in His death and resurrection and the spoils of war are ours.

"I have access to everything the Father made available to Jesus because I am a son, adopted into the family of God. [John 1:12] As an heir, I have free access to operate in the same anointing as Jesus. However, I cannot stop there. I must continue to build on that confidence until it becomes the normal way I live my life. This process destroys the sin consciousness and develops the righteousness consciousness." (Dollar p. 60)

We find our power and our authority in the Word. It is where we get the strength to fight against the enemy and win. We stand upon the scripture and we see the truth there and it makes us bold enough to take on any circumstance, and any devil. We might not appear to be powerful but the One who gave us His victory is.

When a policeman is directing traffic, and puts out his hand signaling "stop," he has no physical means of stopping even the smallest of cars. But because that badge and uniform give him authority, even the driver of an 18 wheeler will downshift and burn up his brakes to stop based on that authority. A hand doesn't mean anything until you recognize the law and the government that enforce that officer's decisions. It is the same with us. On our own we can do nothing, but based on the authority conferred on us, we are powerful. "The value of our authority rests on the power that is behind that authority. God Himself is the power behind our authority! The devil and his forces are obligated to recognize our authority! The believer who thoroughly understands that the power of God is backing him can exercise his authority and face the enemy fearlessly." (Hagin p. 7) We are not doubters, we are believers. As those who believe in the shed blood and the full victory of Christ, we have the right and the responsibility to use His authority to live victoriously on earth until His return.

I Am Who God Says I Am

I Corinthians 1:18 (KJV)
18 For the preaching of the cross is to them that perish foolishness; but unto us which are saved it is the power of God.

Bridging Eternity

The cross of Calvary bridged all of eternity past to all of eternity yet to be seen. It spanned the great sin chasm between God and man. The Lord who hung willingly on that cross joined us forever with a God who loves us. What He did there 2000 years ago is the most important event in your life now. The Lord operates in the realm of the eternal, where neither time nor space is an issue. The whole of time as we know it is within His control. He alone can see the end from the beginning because He is in both places.

Isaiah 46:9-10 (KJV) *9 Remember the former things of old: for I am God, and there is none else; I am God, and there is none like me, 10 Declaring the end from the beginning, and from ancient times the things that are not yet done, saying, My counsel shall stand, and I will do all my pleasure:*

Here on earth, we think of time as linear with everything having a distinct beginning and ending. Where God reigns in the whole of eternity, time is more like a circle and God holds the circle. For Him, all that ever was and ever will be can be firmly grasped at one time. Peter caught sight of the vastness of eternity and said it this way. **II Peter 3:8 (KJV)** *8 But, beloved, be not ignorant of this one thing, that* *one day is with the Lord as a thousand years, and a thousand years as one day.* That thought did not originate with Peter, but was recorded by a psalmist in the Old Testament. **Psalm 90:4 (KJV)** *4 For a thousand years in thy sight are but as yesterday when it is past, and as a watch in the night.* All of the vastness of time can easily be observed in a single glance from the Lord.

Since He is Lord from everlasting to everlasting, God could say that Jesus was a sacrificial lamb given for us before the earth was even created. **Revelation 13:8 (NIV)** *8 All inhabitants of the earth will worship the beast—all whose names have not been written in the Lamb's book of life, the Lamb who was slain from the creation of the world.* God provided for the fallen people of every generation through Jesus. It was accomplished in His heart before the fall. He provided a way of escape for the rebellion of mankind before Adam sinned. The King James Version says that Jesus was the Lamb slain from the foundation of the World. The earth and mankind were yet uncreated but knowing humanity would fall, God prepared to take their place and give unto them—unto us eternal life.

Mankind was in danger, God's beloved was being deceived by the devil and so God sent Christ Jesus, His very own Son. Jesus came in the form of man and to bear the sins of man. He perfectly fulfilled the law. He never once sinned. He who was the spotless Lamb of God took our place so that all of mankind could go free. **I Peter 1:18-21 (NIV)** *18 For you know that it was not with perishable things such as silver or gold that you were redeemed from the empty way of life handed down to you from your ancestors, 19 but with the precious blood of Christ, a lamb without blemish or defect. 20 He was chosen before the creation of the world, but was revealed in these last times for your sake. 21 Through him you* *believe in God, who raised him from the dead and glorified him, and so your faith and hope are in God.*

Jesus was just like every lamb to pay the price of sin from Adam until the final Passover held in Jerusalem that day. When Jesus died, the blood was shed to cleanse men from sin. **Hebrews 9:22 (KJV)** *22 And almost all things are by the law purged with blood; and without shedding of blood is no remission.* Blood paid for freedom for not just a family, or those alive at the time, but for all of mankind. Those standing at the cross could see His precious life blood flow out and fall to the ground that had been cursed because of Adam's sin. They could see the nails in His hands and feet. They could see the pain and the suffering of our Savior. They did not see the millions of the souls under the weight of judgment and sin from the whole of time past until the day of Christ's return, but He could see them. He knew them. Better stated, He knew us, broken and damaged with no hope outside of His blood. Christ's love for us compelled Him to stretch out His hands and endure the whole of the cross for us.

Those people gathered at Calvary could hear the sound of the hammer upon the nail. They could hear His groaning and gasping for air. They did not hear the cry of millions of fallen men begging for the hope of salvation. He heard us. He alone heard the heart of the Father calling back in love. They listened to Him suffering; they could hear others ridicule and insult Him. **Matthew 27:41-45 (KJV)** *41 Likewise also the chief priests mocking him, with the scribes and elders, said, 42 He saved others; himself he cannot save. If he be the King of Israel, let him now come down from the cross, and we will believe him. 43 He trusted in God; let him deliver him now, if he will have him: for he said, I am the Son of God. 44 The thieves also, which were* *crucified with him, cast the same in his teeth. 45 Now from the sixth hour there was darkness over all the land unto the ninth hour.* The Matthew Henry Concise Bible Commentary states the following. "During the three hours in which the darkness continued, Jesus was in agony, wrestling with the powers of darkness, and suffering his Father's displeasure against the sin of man, for which he was now making His soul an offering. Never were there three such hours since the day God created man upon the earth, never such a dark and awful scene; it was the turning point of that great affair, man's redemption and salvation." On the stage of eternity the greatest drama of all time was played out. Mankind was considered worthy of the blood of the Most High, every sin and sinner was held in His heart. Every evil and every broken vessel from every nation was cherished and purchased. God did more at Calvary than any of the men standing there could comprehend. He exchanged the whole of sin for the fullness of grace and made us into sons and daughters.

Those standing at the cross heard the words our Lord spoke. **Luke 23:34 (KJV)** 34 *Then said Jesus, Father, forgive them; for they know not what they do.* Of course, He spoke concerning the soldiers and the rulers of the Temple and the crowds who had cried out for Him to die. Naturally, He prayed for His followers who had scattered and left Him to face the hatred of Rome and the religious leaders. He prayed for the thieves who mocked Him from their own crosses. He who was not bound by time, prayed also for you. When He said, *"Father forgive them for they know not what they do."* He was pleading your case and taking your place. He was bearing your sin and your punishment. He was shedding His holy blood for you. He could see down through time. You were there within Him, being set free. Yes, He looked forward in time as we know it to the lost souls still unborn to make every one of them clean and whole. He also looked back as far as the Garden of Eden. He saw Eve reach for that forbidden fruit, deceived by the devil. He looked as Adam openly chose to rebel against God the Creator who had been his companion. And there at the root of it all, Jesus applied His blood. There where sin and death first took man from unity with the Father the blood flowed freely to cover the whole of mankind's sin. Jesus paid in full for the high price of rejection and independence from God. It was when all of sin was vanquished and the devil lost his hold on mankind that we hear Jesus speak again. **Luke 23:44-46 (KJV)** *44 And it was about the sixth hour, and there was a darkness over all the earth until the ninth hour. 45 And the sun was darkened, and the veil of the temple was rent in the midst. 46 And when Jesus had cried with a loud voice, he said, Father, into thy hands I commend my spirit: and having said thus, he gave up the ghost.*

The whole of mankind was redeemed. Christ had accomplished the will of God. **John 19:30 (KJV)** *30 When Jesus therefore had received the vinegar, he said, It is finished: and he bowed his head, and gave up the ghost.* The final sacrifice was accepted, the sin debt was paid. Mankind had been restored. Jesus had made a way for every man, woman and child ever born to walk with God without condemnation or fear. Jesus had covered us all. According to scripture, when Jesus said, "It is finished." It was not a beaten victim proclaiming His suffering to be done. No! It was the victors cry. Sin is finished. The rebellion is quenched. The animosity between God and man has been bridged. Jesus pulled together all past and future sin and withstood the judgment and penalty they demanded. The sin debt was paid in full.

The centerpiece for time as we know it is the cross of Christ. It intersected time perfectly. The wise men of old even changed how we record time from BC to AD. The sinner could look to the cross and find help and deliverance and salvation at last. There on that cross the old and the new man are exchanged.

Now man is free to be born again. That truth, regarding man's fate, was revealed as Jesus talked with Nicodemus. **John 3: 3 (KJV)** *3 Jesus answered and said unto him, Verily, verily, I say unto thee, Except a man be born again, he cannot see the kingdom of God.* It was the plan and purpose of God to make man a new creation, one without sin and failure, one not separated from His presence. "God sees you in Christ, who is outside time; you step into that timeless zone. In that timeless zone, all your needs and trials are already removed, repaired, restored or resurrected. In that timeless zone in Christ, you are already blessed with every spiritual blessing in the heavenly places! (Prince 10/23/17) **II Corinthians 5:17-19 (KJV)** *17 Therefore if any man be in Christ, he is a new creature: old things are passed away; behold, all things are become new. 18 And all things are of God, who hath reconciled us to himself by Jesus Christ, and hath given to us the ministry of reconciliation; 19 To wit, that God was in Christ, reconciling the world unto himself, not imputing their trespasses unto them;* The new life He poured into us gave us the ability to act in His stead, to carry His name and the accompanying power to do His will on the earth.

God could show the scene at the cross to Isaiah hundreds of years before Jesus was born on earth, because the whole of time was accessible to Him. **Isaiah 53:4-12 (KJV)** *4 Surely he hath borne our griefs, and carried our sorrows: yet we did esteem him stricken, smitten of God, and afflicted. 5 But he was wounded for our transgressions, he was bruised for our iniquities: the chastisement of our peace was upon him; and with his stripes we are healed. 6 All we* *like sheep have gone astray; we have turned every one to his own way; and the LORD hath laid on him the iniquity of us all. 7 He was oppressed, and he was afflicted, yet he opened not his mouth: he is brought as a lamb to the slaughter, and as a sheep before her shearers is dumb, so he openeth not his mouth. 8 He was taken from prison and from judgment: and who shall declare his generation? for he was cut off out of the land of the living: for the transgression of my people was he stricken. 9 And he made his grave with the wicked, and with the rich in his death; because he had done no violence, neither was any deceit in his mouth. 10 Yet it pleased the LORD to bruise him; he hath put him to grief: when thou shalt make his soul an offering for sin, he shall see his seed, he shall prolong his days, and the pleasure of the LORD shall prosper in his hand. 11 He shall see of the travail of his soul, and shall be satisfied: by his knowledge shall my righteous servant justify many; for he shall bear their iniquities. 12 Therefore will I divide him a portion with the great, and he shall divide the spoil with the strong; because he hath poured out his soul unto death: and he was numbered with the transgressors; and he bare the sin of many, and made intercession for the transgressors.* He who knew no sin was made to be sin in our stead and it pleased the Father that now men could believe in the blood once offered and receive salvation. Now God could come near the ones He loved and the only requirement was faith in what Jesus had already accomplished.

I Corinthians 15:22 (KJV) *22 For as in Adam all die, even so in Christ shall all be made alive.* We were all hopelessly sold into sin by the fall. Every person ever born needed a savior. Once saved, we are freed from that bondage. **Romans 5:17 (KJV)** *17 For if by one man's offence death reigned by one; much more they which receive abundance of grace and of the gift of righteousness shall* *reign in life by one, Jesus Christ.* Brother Hagin has this to say concerning that text. "Several translations, including the Amplified Bible, say *reign as kings in life.* Are we just going to reign when we get to heaven? No! We're to reign as kings in life by Jesus Christ. That's authority, isn't it? Whatever the king said was law; he was the last authority. We partake of the authority that Christ's throne represents." (Hagin p.17) His death on the cross gave us access to His power and His kingdom authority.

We have been justified, that is we are made as if we had never sinned and never been part of the fallen world. God declared us to be righteous by virtue of the Blood. Jesus changed us so radically at the new birth that we are now called righteous. **Romans 3:22-24 & 26 (AMP)** *Namely, the righteousness of God which comes by believing with personal trust and confident reliance on Jesus Christ, the Messiah. [And it is meant] for all who believe. For there is no distinction, since all have sinned and are falling short of the honor and glory which God bestows and receives. [All] are justified and made upright and in right standing with God freely and gratuitously by His grace (His unmerited favor and mercy), through the redemption which is [provided] in Christ Jesus...It was to demonstrate and prove at the present time (in the now season) that that He Himself is righteous and that He justified and accepts as righteous him who has [true] faith in Jesus.*

All of our standing with God was purchased for us. We do not and cannot earn right standing with God—it is a gift. Creflo Dollar put it this way. "Years ago, I was shopping at a well-known shoe store and overheard a man who was inquiring about layaway for a pair of shoes he had selected. The Lord spoke to me and said, "Buy those shoes for him." So, I approached the man and asked if those were the shoes he wanted. They were, he replied. I then asked the clerk to wrap them up and give the man his shoes and I would pay for them. However, the man was unable to receive the gift because he couldn't believe that a stranger would actually buy him a pair of shoes. He felt that he had to do something in return for what I had offered. Sadly, he felt he had to earn the gift. He had a problem with receiving. As a result, I could not give it to him even though I really wanted to." (Dollar p.7) What a shame that God had instructed Pastor Dollar and made a way for that man to receive a gift and yet the man would not take it. You are who you are because of what Jesus has done. It is a free gift, but you, much like the man in the store, have to choose to accept the gift.

Romans 10:8-9 (KJV) *8 But what saith it? The word is nigh thee, even in thy mouth, and in thy heart: that is, the word of faith, which we preach; 9 That if thou shalt confess with thy mouth the Lord Jesus, and shalt believe in thine heart that God hath raised him from the dead, thou shalt be saved.* The whole of faith is in that statement; believe in your heart and then confess it openly. Believe and proclaim to see the results of your faith. The Lord wants you saved and He makes it easy to receive His gift.

Acts 2:38 (KJV) *38 Then Peter said unto them, Repent, and be baptized every one of you in the name of Jesus Christ for the remission of sins, and ye shall receive the gift of the Holy Ghost.* While salvation comes to us free, it came at a very high price to God. The Son of God had to die to give you real life. The price for your ransom was not too high for God. He declared that you were worth the whole of it; that price is fully paid and you are free because of it.

The cross is vital to our daily lives. We should be fully aware of the blood shed on the cross and the power transferred there. It is the most powerful, life changing thing that has occurred throughout the whole of time.

I Corinthians 1:18 (KJV) *18 For the preaching of the cross is to them that perish foolishness; but unto us which are saved it is the power of God.* Paul goes on to say that what the world did not recognize in the work of Christ on the cross was more than the wisest men could comprehend. It is only with the help of the Holy Spirit that we can begin to see the amazing power released when Jesus submitted to the Father's will. He became our sacrifice. His blood was shed—His life was extinguished and it released real life, eternal life, to all who would believe.

I Corinthians 2:14 (KJV) *14 But the natural man receiveth not the things of the Spirit of God: for they are foolishness unto him: neither can he know them, because they are spiritually discerned.* All that can be known about God is revealed to those who belong to Him. We were purchased on the cross and birthed into the body of Christ. When we believed that Jesus died for us, and asked for forgiveness based on His sacrifice, we were given the position of sons. As God's own children, we received understanding. We are born again believers with His own Spirit within us. **John 14:26 (KJV)** *26 But the Comforter, which is the Holy Ghost, whom the Father will send in my name, he shall teach you all things, and bring all things to your remembrance, whatsoever I have said unto you.* He will show us truth in the Word of God. Because He authored it, He fully understands it. We as His children have the right to know what the Lord put in the Bible.

God intended that we know our position and walk in truth. Jesus went to the cross to bring us into right standing with the Father. He wants us to freely use the authority He gave us. We are heirs to all that heaven has. Not only are we free from sin, but we belong in the family that reigns over sin and death.

Luke 11:21-22 (KJV) *21 When a strong man armed keepeth his palace, his goods are in peace: 22 But when a stronger than he shall come upon him, and overcome him, he taketh from him all his armour wherein he trusted, and divideth his spoils.*

Binding the Strong Man

Jesus warned us that we would encounter the enemy. When He was on earth, He told the disciples that the devil was a strong adversary. He was not leading them into fear, but into a place where they could put their confidence in His victory.

Luke 11:21-22 (NIV) *21 "When a strong man, fully armed, guards his own house, his possessions are safe .22 But when someone stronger attacks and overpowers him, he takes away the armor in which the man trusted and divides up his plunder.* Without a doubt, Jesus was referring to the fact that for a while the devil had rights of ownership here. That authority, which he had stolen from Adam, was in place. Sin and death and deception reigned here under the devil's dominion for all the years between Adam and Christ. But there was a new Man in town. The time of Satan's rule had ended. Jesus came to take back what Adam had lost. He came with more power and more authority. On the cross, He disarmed the devil.

The devil hopes you don't know that he has been defeated. He has a plan to destroy anyone he can. **John 10:10 (NIV)** *10 The thief comes only to steal and kill and destroy; I have come that they may have life, and have it to* *the full.* The two who fought for the whole of mankind each had a specific role. Satan came to rob you and to bring death and destruction. Jesus came to stand up to that bully and take back all that was and is rightfully yours. He came to give us a full and meaningful and purposeful life.

The devil is no longer a warrior. "He is stripped of his armor of protection. The devil is a confident adversary and completely trusts in his defense. He has faith in the willing obedience of unconverted mankind since Adam sold out to him. He relies on the nagging doubts about God's love and ability to make good His Word to them. We call it unbelief but he accepts it as trust and obedience to him." (Trombley p. 85) He relished the power that he stole from mankind. He ruled ruthlessly; he dominated and controlled sinners. He was a strong man, but his reign was short-lived.

At the time you were saved, at your rebirth, all that the devil had in the way of authority and influence and power was released into your hands. Those symbols of ownership were taken by force at the cross and now they belong to the believer. "Everything Satan possesses, his endowment, prestige, power and authority were all taken from Adam, were converted to Christ's service. Then He distributed them to the new believer. Everything previously used for wickedness and evil is now available for righteousness and is under heavenly authority. The benefits of that victory aren't Christ's (He didn't need them) but ours." (Trombley p. 86) Adam had the nature and character of God. When he let the devil take over, he received the nature of the fallen and death reigned. Now at the new birth, the Nature of God is restored. Men were slaves to Satan, but at salvation, they are born into God's likeness once more. Men become free when they get saved. For the first time since the garden, mankind can take control of their environment. Men can choose because

Jesus defeated that strong man. You are born again from sin. You are not a sinner. You were one, but now you are the redeemed, saved by grace. You were purchased by blood and you are free.

I read long ago that Abraham Lincoln walked past a slave market and saw a young woman on the auction block. She was stripped naked, crying and afraid while evil men bid on her. He was so moved that he went forward and paid for her and then handed her the papers saying that she was free. She did not understand. She thought he owned her and walked along behind him in subjection. He turned to her and said, "You do not belong to me or anyone else. You are free to go wherever you want." When she really understood, she said, "Then since you have been so kind and have given me freedom, I choose to go with you." That should be our response too. Jesus has taken us from bondage and slavery and made us free. Because of what He has done, our hearts should draw us to Him.

The devil had held mankind captive since the fall. He dominated mankind. This cruel taskmaster placed man in spiritual bondage and entangled him with sickness, insecurity, shame and fear. He ruled for a season, but that season has ended. No more can he lead men into sin. **Romans 6:1-18 (KJV)** *1 What shall we say then? Shall we continue in sin, that grace may abound? 2 God forbid. How shall we, that are dead to sin, live any longer therein? 3 Know ye not, that so many of us as were baptized into Jesus Christ were baptized into his death? 4 Therefore we are buried with him by baptism into death: that like as Christ was raised up from the dead by the glory of the Father, even so we also should walk in newness of life. 5 For if we have been planted together in the likeness of his death, we shall be also in the likeness of his resurrection:* This is how we defeat our flesh and keep out of sin. *6 Knowing this, that our old man is crucified with him, that the body of sin might be destroyed, that henceforth we should not serve sin. 7 For he that is dead is freed from sin. 8 Now if we be dead with Christ, we believe that we shall also live with him: 9 Knowing that Christ being raised from the dead dieth no more; death hath no more dominion over him. 10 For in that he died, he died unto sin once: but in that he liveth, he liveth unto God.* We are free when we know what Jesus did and that we were participants in His death and resurrection. We are free to resist any trace of sin. *11 Likewise reckon ye also yourselves to be dead indeed unto sin, but alive unto God through Jesus Christ our Lord. 12 Let not sin therefore reign in your mortal body, that ye should obey it in the lusts thereof.* You refuse to let sin rule and reign. *13 Neither yield ye your members as instruments of unrighteousness unto sin: but yield yourselves unto God, as those that are alive from the dead, and your members as instruments of righteousness unto God.* Remember, you have surrendered your whole life, spirit, soul and body unto God alone. *14 For sin shall not have dominion over you: for ye are not under the law, but under grace. 15 What then? shall we sin, because we are not under the law, but under grace? God forbid. 16 Know ye not, that to whom ye yield yourselves servants to obey, his servants ye are to whom ye obey; whether of sin unto death, or of obedience unto righteousness? 17 But God be thanked, that ye were the servants of sin, but ye have obeyed from the heart that form of doctrine which was delivered you. 18 Being then made free from sin, ye became the servants of righteousness.*

In every legal sense, you have been made free, but you still have to act upon that legal position and take possession of what is yours. It is not enough that Jesus has defeated the enemy and that you can be free; you need to know you are free and walk it out. In Proverbs 23:7 we are told that *"As a man thinks, so is he."* If you think and act as if you are free, you truly are, but on the contrary, if you believe you are still in bondage, you will never walk in total freedom.

Hebrews 2:14-15 (KJV) *14 Forasmuch then as the children are partakers of flesh and blood, he also himself likewise took part of the same; that through death he might destroy him that had the power of death, that is, the devil; 15 And deliver them who through fear of death were all their lifetime subject to bondage.* Jesus came as a man and resisted all sin and every lure of the world. Then He willingly went to the cross to pay in full for sin. The total accumulation of all that was evil was embodied in Christ. Jesus suffered as if He was guilty, but it was acquired sin, our sin. We were sinners, failures in life until He hung there as our substitute. He died in our place. He hung there on that cross, between heaven and hell, and reached out His hands in love for us. He made a bridge so we could get back to God.

Colossians 2:13-15 (KJV) *13 And you, being dead in your sins and the uncircumcision of your flesh, hath he quickened together with him, having forgiven you all trespasses; 14 Blotting out the handwriting of ordinances that was against us, which was contrary to us, and took it out of the way, nailing it to his cross; 15 And having spoiled principalities and powers, he made a shew of them openly, triumphing over them in it.* The new birth was not a small thing. It was a conquering of an evil dictator and a transfer of both authority and nature. We are not just dusted off and shined up. We are completely new, fully acceptable to God. We are welcome in God's house. Think of it like this. "Satan stood speechless as Jesus walked quickly to the gates of Paradise. Behind those ancient gates was a large crowd of faithful believers, held captive by Satan as long as he held the keys of death. They were expecting Jesus....Jesus slipped the key of authority into the lock and opened it for the first time, since Adam fell. (Trombley p. 101) **Ephesians 4:8 (KJV)** *8 ... he led captivity captive.* Adam walked out free; Abraham and David came out free. And down through the ages all who died waiting for the Messiah were able to finally walk out of that place. And since then no believer has had to wait for redemption. It is already ours.

      The Lord holds the key and He has opened wide the door to freedom. "Jesus systematically stripped the defeated Satan before all the host of heaven, and earth and hell. He was not allowed to retain even the weakest aspect of authority, or recognition, lest he make a second claim." (Trombley p. 104) You are given the victory that Jesus won. The devil has nothing left to fight with. His only tool is deception. He would have you to believe he is powerful, but he is a loser. Satan is defeated. All of his destruction has been undone. His dominance is ended. He has been rendered useless and ineffective. The devil has been permanently dethroned, and through Christ you are now stronger than he is.

I Am Who God Says I Am

I Peter 5:8-9 (KJV) *8 Be sober, be vigilant; because your adversary the devil, as a roaring lion, walketh about, seeking whom he may devour: 9 Whom resist stedfast in the faith, knowing that the same afflictions are accomplished in your brethren that are in the world.*

Dead Lions

Sometimes I think that believers, who are on their way to heaven, act more like they are heading down the path to Oz saying, "Lions and tigers and bears, oh my." They are bound by fear and troubled by all the devil throws their way.

I Peter 5:8 (KJV) *8 Be sober, be vigilant; because your adversary the devil, as a roaring lion, walketh about, seeking whom he may devour:* That scripture doesn't say he is a lion; he comes acting like he is a lion. The devil masquerades as a lion, he is playing dress up. He comes to attack, but the faker cannot destroy those who belong to God.

Let's talk for a moment about lions. When lions are hunting, the pack works together to defeat their prey. The oldest and weakest of the lions roars to frighten the prey into running away. The strong, young lion doesn't do the roaring; he hides along the path leading away from the old, decrepit, roaring lion. The most dangerous lions just lie in wait. The smartest thing to do would be to run toward the roar. That one that threatens is not even dangerous. The devil comes roaring but he has been rendered powerless.

Not too many of us have ever had to fight a real lion. Some have, among them was Daniel. Because he was faithful to God, Daniel was thrown into the lion's den and left there until morning. God shut the mouth of those lions and the servant of God just lay down and slept with them. They were real lions and they were hungry, but they had no power over him. **Daniel 6:16-17 (KJV)** *16 Then the king commanded, and they brought Daniel, and cast him into the den of lions. Now the king spake and said unto Daniel, Thy God whom thou servest continually, he will deliver thee. 17 And a stone was brought, and laid upon the mouth of the den; and the king sealed it with his own signet, and with the signet of his lords; that the purpose might not be changed concerning Daniel.* His life must have been quite a testimony to inspire such faith in king Darius.

Scripture tells us the king fasted and in the morning went and cried out asking if God had indeed protected this man of integrity. **Daniel 6:22-24 (KJV)** *22 My God hath sent his angel, and hath shut the lions' mouths, that they have not hurt me: forasmuch as before him innocency was found in me; and also before thee, O king, have I done no hurt. 23 Then was the king exceeding glad for him, and commanded that they should take Daniel up out of the den. So Daniel was taken up out of the den, and no manner of hurt was found upon him, because he believed in his God. 24 And the king commanded, and they brought those men which had accused Daniel, and they cast them into the den of lions, them, their children, and their wives; and the lions had the mastery of them, and brake all their bones in pieces or ever they came at the bottom of the den.* Those very strong and very hungry lions were under the control of a more powerful God. God was <u>with</u> Daniel, but more importantly, He lives in you.

Samson also defeated a lion. **Judges 14:5-6 (KJV)** *5 ... behold, a young lion roared against him. 6 And the Spirit* *of the LORD came mightily upon him, and he rent him as he would have rent a kid, and he had nothing in his hand...* When that very real lion, which was the most ferocious of beasts, came to attack an Old Testament man with just a taste of the power you have, Samson tore it apart. You have that kind of power to stop the fake spiritual lion, the lie of the devil, and kill it when it comes to get you.

David said he fought both a lion and bear. **I Samuel 17:34-37 (KJV)** *Thy servant kept his father's sheep, and there came a lion, and a bear, and took a lamb out of the flock: 35 And I went out after him, and smote him, and delivered it out of his mouth: and when he arose against me, I caught him by his beard, and smote him, and slew him. 36 Thy servant slew both the lion and the bear: and this uncircumcised Philistine shall be as one of them, seeing he hath defied the armies of the living God. 37 David said moreover, The LORD that delivered me out of the paw of the lion, and out of the paw of the bear, he will deliver me out of the hand of this Philistine.* David knew the power of God could stop any enemy. Those natural lions were sent by the devil to take out those men of God and they failed every time.

The devil does come around roaring at us trying to scare us. He bites at us with sickness and disease and wants to hurt us and even kill us, but he can't. He wants you afraid of him, running from him, but you don't have to fear anything, not even death.

Look how Jesus handled the devil when the lion of sickness and death came roaring to the house of Lazarus. He was sick and then died, but Jesus was more powerful than the any sickness, more powerful than death. **John 11:41-42 (KJV)** 41 *Then they took away the stone from the place where the dead was laid. And Jesus lifted up his eyes,* *and said, Father, I thank thee that thou hast heard me. 42 And I knew that thou hearest me always: but because of the people which stand by I said it, that they may believe that thou hast sent me.* When did God hear Him? He heard Jesus say, *"This sickness will not end in death."* God also heard Him say, *"I go to wake him."* God heard Jesus tell Martha, *"I am the resurrection and the life. Your brother will live again."* Every time the lion of death came to the door, Jesus answered with faith and each of those times His words of life were sown into the atmosphere. Jesus had been preparing for this moment with every word He spoke. **John 11:43** *43 And when he thus had spoken, he cried with a loud voice, Lazarus, come forth. 44 And he that was dead came forth, bound hand and foot with graveclothes: and his face was bound about with a napkin. Jesus saith unto them, Loose him, and let him go.* The grave clothes didn't belong on him. The stench of death and decay had no place on him. The trappings of death have no place on you either.

Jesus stood between men and that old lion over and over. He healed the sick, raised the dead daughter of Jairus and the son of the widow. He openly stopped sickness and disease in their tracks. He stood victorious against every attack of the enemy upon mankind so the devil threw his best punch—death. An angry crowd took Jesus to the cross. They nailed Him there for my sin, my failure, and my sickness. He willingly took my place. When the Lord was on the cross he quoted the whole of this chapter about his crucifixion look what he says. **Psalm 22:13 (KJV)** *13 They gaped upon me with their mouths, as a ravening and a roaring lion.* The devil came attacking Jesus, his mouth open ready to rip and devour His flesh. The devil roared as if he had power. He incited a riotous crowd to demand the Lord be crucified. He stood by to make sure Jesus was dead, but death was not enough to stop our Lord.

Galatians 2:20 (KJV) *20 I am crucified with Christ: nevertheless I live; yet not I, but Christ liveth in me: and the life which I now live in the flesh I live by the faith of the Son of God, who loved me, and gave himself for me.* Sin was crucified; sickness was crucified. Death died. Jesus bore them all, took them to the cross and saw them forever destroyed. He was the sacrifice who took our place, paid our full debt, suffered all we should have suffered and when Justice was complete in Him he said, "It is finished."

He did not stay there. Friday was awful. Every disciple felt defeated, but Sunday was coming. Jesus arose, the first alive from the dead. He had met the claims of justice. Therefore, He was able to give that resurrection life, that eternal life to others.

Early Sunday morning, Mary had found the grave open, empty. Jesus no longer lay there in apparent defeat. The words she spoke stirred up questions. Was Christ's body removed, or had He really risen? Peter and John came to see if it was true that He was gone. **John 20:4-9 (KJV)** *4 So they ran both together: and the other disciple did outrun Peter, and came first to the sepulchre. 5 And he stooping down, and looking in, saw the linen clothes lying; yet went he not in. 6 Then cometh Simon Peter following him, and went into the sepulchre, and seeth the linen clothes lie, 7 And the napkin, that was about his head, not lying with the linen clothes, but wrapped together in a place by itself. 8 Then went in also that other disciple, which came first to the sepulchre, and he saw, and believed. 9 For as yet they knew not the scripture, that he must rise again from the dead.* John saw something that changed him, made a believer out of him. There where the master's body had lain, where sin was buried, lay an empty shroud.

That scene makes more sense when you realize how they buried our Lord and what those two men actually saw. They did not embalm Jesus' body but they wrapped it in linen cloth. The Jews, like the Egyptians, used a sticky, mixture to cover the flesh that included myrrh and aloes. Then thin strips of cloth were smeared with that substance and wrapped around the body. That substance weighed about 100 pounds and quickly hardened. [See John 19:39-42] The body looked similar to what you see in the Mummy movies. They covered all but His face with those strips. It was the face that Mary intended to finish after the Sabbath when she arrived at the tomb. The face was covered with a separate cloth; John called it a napkin. The text says Jesus was not there; the tomb was empty. More importantly, that cocoon or shell of grave clothes was empty. Only a miracle could have left it as it was. That covering had hardened, like a plaster cast; no one could have removed the body without damaging it. It was still there, just an empty shell. Either Jesus at the resurrection had come through the whole of that shell or had left through the tiny face opening. That is why John believed the Lord had risen. The face cloth was not just discarded, but neatly folded and laying nearby. [John20:7] That was also symbolic to the disciples.

I once heard a Jewish Rabbi speak. He said that any thankful guest in a Jewish home knew how to signal his gratitude. Instead of crumpling his used napkin and leaving it on the table, the guest would neatly fold and lay aside his napkin apart from where he had been seated. That would show that he had been honored to be in the house and that he would come again to visit. If we follow that train of thought, Jesus was saying, "I am glad I had time with you, and I want to spend more time with you; I will return." His face napkin folded and lying in a place nearby was a powerful statement.

John saw the grave clothes and he believed Jesus was alive; Jesus had risen from the dead. John went into that tomb spiritually dead. He stared at death's domain. John saw the trappings of death, now empty and when he did, John walked out alive. I want to repeat that for emphasis. John went into the tomb, that place of the dead, and realized Jesus was alive. Then John, who was dead when he went in, took on that resurrected life—He believed, and because of that, life poured into him too. John was now a live man inside the grave and the devil knew there was no more hope of stopping Jesus or the ones who loved Him. Death had been defeated in Christ and because of that its power was destroyed in us. We would never have to fear it again.

Hebrews 2:14-15 (KJV) *14 Forasmuch then as the children are partakers of flesh and blood, he also himself likewise took part of the same; that through death he might destroy him that had the power of death, that is, the devil; 15 And deliver them who through fear of death were all their lifetime subject to bondage.*

There is nothing more dead than death. There is nothing sicker, weaker or more devastated than sickness and disease. Jesus took their power; He defeated their creator and has weakened their hold. All they can do is roar like a toothless lion, and try to scare you. They have no destruction left in them.

That old fraud, the devil, thought he had defeated Jesus and us. The cross he used to attempt to solidify his hold on humanity was not an execution but rather a release for all the ones held captive. The vertical beam of the cross was reaching toward God and the horizontal one reaching out to man. Jesus used that cross to bridge the gap and allowed us access to all that is God's. We might live on foreign soil, but we are protected and provided for by the King.

"Have you ever wondered why besides holding a whip, the trainer would arm himself with a stool and point its legs toward the beast? The whole idea is to distract the lion. You see, as powerful as the beast is, it can be immobilized by distractions. If this man-eater is not distracted from time to time, it might maul the trainer to death. The devil is like the trainer. He knows that you have God's power inside you because the lion of Judah is in you. *Greater is he who is in you than he that is in the world.* So what the devil tries to do is immobilize you with distractions." (Prince 9/16/17) Whatever gets your attention off of your victory in Christ gives him an advantage. The devil wants you to look at the problem, look at the sickness or the need. He wants you focused on anything but the power of God. "God wants you to focus on who you are and what you have in Christ." (Prince 9/16/17) When you are fully conscious that you are the healed, the overcomer, the saved, the redeemed you will trust in the power of God and go free.

Jesus is the Lion of the tribe of Judah, crowned with power and glory. The reason the devil came disguised as a lion is that he wanted to be God and couldn't; he wanted you to think he was all powerful when he wasn't. We won't fall for it, because we have seen the real thing.

Look at what God says about the believers who put their trust in Him. **Psalm 91:9-16 (KJV)** *9 Because thou hast made the LORD, which is my refuge, even the most High, thy habitation; 10 There shall no evil befall thee, neither shall any plague come nigh thy dwelling. 11 For he shall give his angels charge over thee, to keep thee in all thy ways. 12 They shall bear thee up in their hands, lest thou* *dash thy foot against a stone. 13 Thou shalt tread upon the lion and adder: the young lion and the dragon shalt thou trample under feet. 14 Because he hath set his love upon me, therefore will I deliver him: I will set him on high, because he hath known my name. 15 He shall call upon me, and I will answer him: I will be with him in trouble; I will deliver him, and honour him. 16 With long life will I satisfy him, and shew him my salvation.*

You might think you are weak and that you have no hope, but check this out. **Ecclesiastes 9:4 (NIV)** *4 Anyone who is among the living has hope—even a live dog is better off than a dead lion!* That devil is a dead lion. You are more than enough to defeat him. While you are here on the earth you have the same opportunity as John. You can recognize that Jesus died for you; Jesus rose from the dead. When you believe in His finished work of redemption, you can be born again. Once you are alive in Him that old lion the devil is no match for you.

Do you want to know what happened to that fake lion, the devil, who came with sickness and death and tried to take you out? **Job 4:10-11 (KJV)** *10 The roaring of the lion, and the voice of the fierce lion, and the teeth of the young lions, are broken. 11 The old lion perisheth for lack of prey, and the stout lion's whelps are scattered abroad.* He has no bite, no power, and no ability to destroy you; it is all roar. Even his little demons are scattered. The devil wanted you to believe you were easy prey but you are not. That devil is nothing but a roaring lion, seeking someone to devour. The Lion of the Tribe of Judah is Jesus, He is for you. That old toothless thing roaring after you is the devil. My friend, Donna, says, "Let him roar; its falling on deaf ears." Why would we be afraid of a dead shell of a thing? You belong to Jesus and He has defeated the devil.

He defeated sickness and sin and death and He has given you His very Life. According to Trombley, Jesus could have said it this way to the devil. "I am the Lion of the tribe of Judah, and I am conferring my authority to my children. When they use my name against you, you would be wise to flee from them as quickly as possible. The weakest, the frailest, the most timid one among them is much greater than you. All my authority, power, creative ability and immortality stand against you…I AM. Now get out of my presence, and don't forget Satan, keep looking over your shoulder!" (Trombley p. 105)

I Peter 5:6-9 (KJV) *6 Humble yourselves therefore under the mighty hand of God, that he may exalt you in due time: 7 Casting all your care upon him; for he careth for you. Surrender the whole of your life to the One who bought it. 8 Be sober, be vigilant; because your adversary the devil, as a roaring lion, walketh about, seeking whom he may devour:* The Amplified Bible says he roars in fierce hunger, seeking someone to seize and devour. Therefore, you withstand him! Be firm in faith against his onset. Be rooted and established, strong, immovable and determined because you and the overcomer are one! That dumb shell of a thing wants to eat you up, but the Lord has told us how to handle him. *9Whom resist stedfast in the faith, knowing that the same afflictions are accomplished in your brethren that are in the world.*

When he comes at you—he finds the true Lion of the tribe of Judah who has already overcome death. That stupid fake lion finds an army of life-filled ones who are not within his power to destroy. He sees you free from all the trappings of death, there is no stench of sin or death on you. The devil has no real power over you.

Jesus already defeated your enemy. Jesus is alive. You are alive in Him and He is alive in you. What about the devil? Jesus has stripped him of all power and authority. The devil is just playing dress up, appearing to be strong when he is just wearing the skin of a dead lion.

II Corinthians 5:17-18 (KJV)
17 Therefore if any man be in Christ, he is a new creature: old things are passed away; behold, all things are become new. 18 And all things are of God, who hath reconciled us to himself by Jesus Christ,

In Christ

We do not stand by our own goodness or ability, but all that we are is based on the fact that we are included in Christ's work of redemption. God did a work in Christ that included all future believers. Everything that we are, was created in that blood sacrifice that gave us entrance into the presence of God and new life. We are His, purchased and rebirthed through His obedience and suffering. He made us righteous and wise and good. He placed within us compassion and any other good characteristic that might be found in us. **Ephesians 1:17-23 (KJV)** *17 That the God of our Lord Jesus Christ, the Father of glory, may give unto you the spirit of wisdom and revelation in the knowledge of him:* Paul prayed that the believers would gain wisdom and knowledge and understanding about the fullness of their redemption and relationship with the Lord. *18 The eyes of your understanding being enlightened; that ye may know what is the hope of his calling, and what the riches of the glory of his inheritance in the saints, 19 And what is the exceeding greatness of his power to us-ward who believe, according to the working of his mighty power, 20 Which he wrought in Christ, when he raised him from the dead, and set him at his own right hand in the heavenly places, 21 Far above all principality, and power, and might, and dominion, and every name that is named, not only in this world, but also* *in that which is to come: 22 And hath put all things under his feet, and gave him to be the head over all things to the church, 23 Which is his body, the fulness of him that filleth all in all.* The full authority we have is in our relationship with Him.

Our partnership with Jesus and our faith in Him will be distributed and become effective, powerful, active, and operational through knowing and walking in all the good things we have in Christ. If we are in Christ, what does that mean? It means that we are the saved, the true believers and the ones who are members of the body, but there is more. The word Christ means both the Anointed One and His anointing. If we come in the name of Jesus the Christ, we are coming in the name of the One who is anointed and we come within His anointing. We are bearing the same anointing that He presented. I found 77 places in the New Testament that used the phrase "in Christ." There are many more that support our position within the anointed body of believers. Our whole life is hidden in Him. I heard Kenneth Copeland say that every time you see the word Christ you should mentally substitute the Anointed One and His anointing to keep the fullness of the message.

God did the entire work of salvation, regeneration and deliverance in what happened on the cross and within the resurrected Christ who came out of the tomb. He who overcame death is able to give that new life to us as believers. **I Corinthians 15:21-22 (KJV)** *21 For since by man came death, by man came also the resurrection of the dead. 22 For as in Adam all die, even so in Christ shall all be made alive.* We are either in Christ, in the Anointed One and His Anointing or we are not. All those who are saved have been included in Christ; we are the redeemed and we represent Him on earth.

Romans 8:1 (KJV) *1 There is therefore now no condemnation to them which are in Christ Jesus, who walk not after the flesh, but after the Spirit.* The Father God included us in what Jesus did. He put us within the Sacrificial Lamb. There is no sense of shame in the true believer. Because the one who failed God died on the cross, within the heart of Christ Jesus. Yes we try to live well, because we are His, but we do not have to work at anything because we are included in His sacrifice and in His triumph over sin and death. We were as much a part of the body of Christ while Jesus was dying as we are now. We just didn't know it. **Romans 8:2 (KJV)** *2 For the law of the Spirit of life in Christ Jesus hath made me free from the law of sin and death.* The power and authority in the Anointed One has set us free. That authority and power was in Him, and it is still in the anointing that we walk in. Our debt was paid, in Him. Our hope was secured in Him.

Our earthly bodies and frail emotions are host to the power and the anointing that exists in Him. **II Corinthians 4:6-7 (KJV)** *6 For God, who commanded the light to shine out of darkness, hath shined in our hearts, to give the light of the knowledge of the glory of God in the face of Jesus Christ. 7 But we have this treasure in earthen vessels, that the excellency of the power may be of God, and not of us.* We carry His anointing and no matter how flawed we are, the glory of God is housed in us.

II Corinthians 5:17-21 (KJV) *17 Therefore if any man be in Christ, he is a new creature: old things are passed away; behold, all things are become new. 18 And all things are of God, who hath reconciled us to himself by Jesus Christ, and hath given to us the ministry of reconciliation; 19 To wit, that God was in Christ, reconciling the world unto himself, not imputing their trespasses unto them; and hath* *committed unto us the word of reconciliation. 20 Now then we are ambassadors for Christ, as though God did beseech you by us: we pray you in Christ's stead, be ye reconciled to God. 21 For he hath made him to be sin for us, who knew no sin; that we might be made the righteousness of God in him.* We have identified with the Lord. We became one with Him. We arose victorious in Him. Now we walk in His anointing.

All that Christ [the Anointed One and His anointing] did was intentionally done for us. **Ephesians 1:3 (KJV)** *3 Blessed be the God and Father of our Lord Jesus Christ, who hath blessed us with all spiritual blessings in heavenly places in Christ:* All that was sinful or evil or weakened by the fall was laid on Him; sickness, sin, rebellion and failure died there on the cross. "We are no longer at the cross. We died with Christ, but He has raised us up together with Him. Glory to God; learn how to take your place of authority. The right hand of the throne of God is the center of power for the whole universe! Exercising the power of the throne was committed to the resurrected Lord." (Hagin p. 16) We are to live in full awareness of His great victory and in freedom because we are not outside observers, but participants in that victory. We are vessels of His power and anointing, continuing His work.

Paul was praying for his friend in Christ. **Philemon 1:6 (KJV)** *6 That the communication of thy faith may become effectual by the acknowledging of every good thing which is in you in Christ Jesus.* All that we are, and all we accomplish, is because of our relationship with Christ. Every good thing in us is birthed from Him and through Him. Our faith and love should bind us together much stronger than any earthly family. He has made us one body, completely and permanently concealed within the dying Lamb and the resurrected Lord Jesus. Paul asked Philemon to recognize the brother that he had gained in the salvation of his former slave. He said that while he had been wronged and defrauded prior to this, the new birth made him both joined to and equal to the one he had owned. **Romans 12:4-5 (KJV)** *4 For as we have many members in one body, and all members have not the same office: 5 So we, being many, are one body in Christ, and every one members one of another.* Unity with the saved of this world is not an option we are one body, united. There is no racial difference, no gender difference, no class system in the body; we all belong to Him and in Him, and are a part of Him. **Galatians 3:26-29 (KJV)** *26 For ye are all the children of God by faith in Christ Jesus. 27 For as many of you as have been baptized into Christ have put on Christ.* Notice it says here that you have put on the anointing. *28 There is neither Jew nor Greek, there is neither bond nor free, there is neither male nor female: for ye are all one in Christ Jesus. 29 And if ye be Christ's, then are ye Abraham's seed, and heirs according to the promise.* There should be no jealousy or division in the church; we are the body of Christ. His blood and His anointing are great equalizers. We are all in Him and operate in His continuous power and anointing.

Luke 4:16-21 (KJV) *16 And he came to Nazareth, where he had been brought up: and, as his custom was, he went into the synagogue on the sabbath day, and stood up for to read. 17 And there was delivered unto him the book of the prophet Esaias. And when he had opened the book, he found the place where it was written, 18 The Spirit of the Lord is upon me, because he hath anointed me to preach the gospel to the poor; he hath sent me to heal the brokenhearted, to preach deliverance to the captives, and recovering of sight to the blind, to set at liberty them that are bruised, 19 To preach the acceptable year of the Lord. 20 And he closed the* *book, and he gave it again to the minister, and sat down. And the eyes of all them that were in the synagogue were fastened on him. 21 And he began to say unto them, This day is this scripture fulfilled in your ears.* His claim was the anointing; your claim is the anointing. That anointing is what causes us as believers to be able to preach, to heal, and to minister as He did. It was His command in Mark 16:15-18 for us to walk out our union with Him. His anointing in us would qualify and empower us to do the work.

I Corinthians 1:2 (KJV) *2 Unto the church of God which is at Corinth, to them that are sanctified in Christ Jesus, called to be saints, with all that in every place call upon the name of Jesus Christ our Lord, both theirs and ours:* If we call upon the name of our Lord Jesus we are joined together. We are one with the Father and one with each other and that oneness produces a powerful manifestation of His presence in the earth. Jesus died to make it possible for us to stand as one family of reborn children. All that we will ever need was accomplished on the cross of Calvary. We were there in His heart, our lives were forever changed while the blood flowed from His wounds and the anointing that had been in Him became our inheritance. There are treasures of wisdom and knowledge that we have not even begun to touch, but they are available to us in Christ. **Colossians 2:2-3 (KJV)** *2 That their hearts might be comforted, being knit together in love, and unto all riches of the full assurance of understanding, to the acknowledgement of the mystery of God, and of the Father, and of Christ; 3 In whom are hid all the treasures of wisdom and knowledge.* All the hidden mysteries are open for us to search out now that we are His. Jesus promised that the Holy Spirit would reveal them to us.

Paul said **I Corinthians 2:2 (KJV)** *2 For I determined not to know anything among you, save Jesus Christ, and him* *crucified.* The Anointed One and His anointing are enough to make us overcomers. Jesus the Anointed One is alive and still at work in believers. Paul said, 'I have decided to put one truth above all others. I know only this that Jesus is Lord, that He is the Son of God. He was crucified on the cross. I focus on the cross and all the benefits of His shed blood.' Paul was smart enough to realize that all his prior education and standing in the community were nothing. He gave himself to one thing only. [Phil 3:13] Paul determined to let the cross affect all he did and said. He focused on the power and presence of the Holy Spirit through the perfect sacrifice of Jesus; he believed in a resurrected Christ. He believed the anointing was still present in all who were joined to the Lord. Paul cherished the Lord and the power present in the anointing; he walked in it. He took hold of salvation, healing, deliverance, peace and prosperity because they were all part of the benefit package. He did not allow any part of his old life to keep the resurrection out of him.

Salvation is only in Christ and when we remember that, we can tolerate a lot more in this world. **II Timothy 1:9-10(KJV)** *9 Who hath saved us, and called us with an holy calling, not according to our works, but according to his own purpose and grace, which was given us in Christ Jesus before the world began, 10 Therefore I endure all things for the elect's sakes, that they may also obtain the salvation which is in Christ Jesus with eternal glory.* Paul instructed Timothy concerning the evil in the world and told him that in order to make it through we had to cling to our union with Jesus and our union with all Christians and to cling to the wisdom and knowledge that comes to us through faith in Christ. We believe in the One who was anointed and we choose to live as the anointed, sharing His life and power and victory with all the other believers. It will not be a smooth ride. **II Timothy 3:12-15 (KJV)** *12 Yea, and all* *that will live godly in Christ Jesus shall suffer persecution. 13 But evil men and seducers shall wax worse and worse, deceiving, and being deceived. 14 But continue thou in the things which thou hast learned and hast been assured of, knowing of whom thou hast learned them; 15 And that from a child thou hast known the holy scriptures, which are able to make thee wise unto salvation through faith which is in Christ Jesus.* Cling to the truth. Hold fast to the scriptures and the blood. It is enough to make you strong in faith and able to overcome. **I John 4:4 (KJV)** *4 Ye are of God, little children, and have overcome them: because greater is he that is in you, than he that is in the world.*

Christians are not promised an easy road. There will be danger, and problems, but the Lord will see us through them all. **Romans 8:37-39 (KJV)** *37 Nay, in all these things we are more than conquerors through him that loved us. 38 For I am persuaded, that neither death, nor life, nor angels, nor principalities, nor powers, nor things present, nor things to come, 39 Nor height, nor depth, nor any other creature, shall be able to separate us from the love of God, which is in Christ Jesus our Lord.* There is no power in the spirit or in the realm of the natural that can touch us. We are in Christ. We have been made righteous, made victorious. We walk in the fullness of His anointing and share in His perfect love. Believers do not need to strive for anything.

John 14:19-20 (KJV) *19 Yet a little while, and the world seeth me no more; but ye see me: because I live, ye shall live also. 20 At that day ye shall know that I am in my Father, and ye in me, and I in you.* We carry His DNA, His anointing; we look just like Him in the spirit. We are now included in the unity that existed within the trinity throughout all of eternity past. It is that unity that makes us overcomers in life. We walk in the shadow of the Almighty. We have a big brother, standing just over our shoulder, and any enemy would have to fight Him to get to us. All that I need is in Christ. I am in Him and He and the Father are in me. What an awesome thing that I might be part of His body and His bride. I abide within the Anointed One and His anointing.

Ephesians 6:10-11 (KJV)

10 Finally, my brethren, be strong in the Lord, and in the power of his might. 11 Put on the whole armour of God, that ye may be able to stand against the wiles of the devil.

Dressed for Success

Believers are to be clothed with spiritual armor. It is not something we wear occasionally, but our standard uniform as members of His army. We do spiritual battle when we continue the ministry Christ began. We are dressed for success, because we are covered in every area the devil wants to attack us. "Christ's triumphant victory was more than just defeating sin, unrighteousness, and death subjectively, but objectively bringing to birth true righteousness, life and fellowship. His violent regaining of the Kingdom was more than merely dethroning Satan, but occupying the realms of his dominion and reoccupying the places he held by usurped authority." (Trombley p. 27) We never have to go head to head against the devil because he is already defeated, but by faith we do enforce the Lord's victory.

Paul was a prisoner chained to a Roman soldier when he wrote the letter to the church in Ephesus. He won many of those soldiers to Christ, but while he was there writing, he used their armor and weapons to illustrate ours. **Ephesians 6:10-18 (KJV)** *10 Finally, my brethren, be strong in the Lord, and in the power of his might. 11 Put on the whole armour of God, that ye may be able to stand against the wiles of the devil. 12 For we wrestle not against flesh and blood, but against principalities, against powers, against the rulers of* *the darkness of this world, against spiritual wickedness in high places. 13 Wherefore take unto you the whole armour of God, that ye may be able to withstand in the evil day, and having done all, to stand. 14 Stand therefore, having your loins girt about with truth, and having on the breastplate of righteousness; 15 And your feet shod with the preparation of the gospel of peace; 16 Above all, taking the shield of faith, wherewith ye shall be able to quench all the fiery darts of the wicked. 17 And take the helmet of salvation, and the sword of the Spirit, which is the word of God: 18 Praying always with all prayer and supplication in the Spirit, and watching thereunto with all perseverance and supplication for all saints;*

Each of the pieces of armor represents an area of strong defense against our enemy, and an area he would like to attack. The first is the belt of truth. [Verse 14] We must know the Word of God and the power contained in it. We will not easily fall for a lie, a distraction or deception if we have been grounded in the truth. The Roman soldier wore a six to eight inch wide leather belt that tied every other part of the armor together and it is the truth in the Word of God that encircles us to keep us protected. "If his belt slipped in battle, he would become vulnerable. Our belt is the truth of God's Word. All our combat equipment stands or falls with it. The truth refers specifically to our knowledge and understanding of the Bible. A soldier could not wait until he was already in the battle to put on his belt. Neither can we wait to learn the Scripture." (Lindsey p. 184) I also like to think of this as protecting our reproductive area. If I am full of the truth, I am likely to birth new members into the body of Christ.

Trombley believed that all of the protective gear named in this chapter was indeed the Word. He said that the enemy would like to attack you with doubt, just like he came to Eve. "Has God really said?" If we are saturated with the Word of God we will know what God has and has not said. Satan is deceptive and one of his most effective weapons is half-truths. Satan wants us to rationalize and justify our lack of faith and our sins. He will try to distort and manipulate the Scriptures so that his distortion seems reasonable. Forget reasonable, the Word is truth and nothing but the truth. Do not add or subtract from it. Don't let your mind be idle or wander; focus on the truth and let it cover your vital organs.

In verse 14 it also says we have a breastplate of righteousness. Where did we get it? It was part of the great exchange. **II Corinthians 5:21 (KJV)** *21 For he hath made him to be sin for us, who knew no sin; that we might be made the righteousness of God in him.* What I was has been replaced by His nature and His character. I was made righteous by faith. It was unearned and yet it was freely given. Since God sees me as righteous, justified and pure by virtue of the blood, I just agree with Him and stand without guilt or shame. "The breastplate was made of bronze backed with tough pieces of leather." (Lindsey p. 184) The Word of God assures me I am saved and sanctified and righteous, because Jesus bestowed those attributes on me. I cling to that view of myself and my heart is well covered.

The next article of clothing is a covering for our feet. It represents the ability to stand, so we do not easily slip or lose balance. It also represents our ability to keep marching forward against all opposition. "The Roman soldier was issued hobnail sandals so that he could keep a sure footing… In our battle with the devil, sure footing is even more important." (Lindsey p. 185) Rather than army boots, think of it as a preparation for us to constantly be marching into the enemy camp with the gospel that men can be saved. The

Word keeps us standing firmly on a strong foundation and faithfully proclaiming the Word of God and the testimony of Christ's victory. I like it that there is a scripture that say I have beautiful feet. **Romans 10:15 (KJV)** *...as it is written, How beautiful are the feet of them that preach the gospel of peace, and bring glad tidings of good things!*

Then the Scripture says to take the shield of faith. A shield is defensive protection. In the Roman army shields were large enough to cover the soldier completely. There were some shields that almost looked like a door, and if soldiers stood side by side they made a wall of defense. Take faith and actively use it to defend yourself and your brothers in arms. Stand close to other believers and make your position impenetrable. **Hebrews 10:25 (KJV)** *25 Not forsaking the assembling of ourselves together, as the manner of some is; but exhorting one another: and so much the more, as ye see the day approaching.* The text in Ephesians 6:16 says *Above all, taking the shield of faith, wherewith ye shall be able to quench all the fiery darts of the wicked;* we can use our faith to snuff out the fiery darts of our enemy. We can block his every attack. "Faith works only as you aggressively act upon every promise in the word. You believe the Word; therefore, you act upon it." (Trombley p. 129) Acting on the Word we believe brings us to the Sword of the Spirit. He said take the Word in hand and use it to intentionally take ground from the enemy. This is our only offensive weapon. "It is more than mental acceptance, verbal agreement or silent hoping, but a RHEMA, which is the spoken word. As far as the devil is concerned, this is the most offensive weapon the believer has." (Trombley p. 130) Fill yourself up on the Word and it will come out of your mouth. **Luke 6:45 (KJV)** *45 A good man out of the good treasure of his heart bringeth forth that which is good; and an evil man out of the evil treasure of his heart bringeth forth that which is evil: for of the abundance* *of the heart his mouth speaketh.* "Only when the word has become part of you can you say it as a RHEMA, the sword of the Lord. It is more than the quoted Word, more than the printed word, more than the listened to word, it is the absorbed Word." (Trombley p. 130) When you speak the Word of God with authority the devil hears the voice of Jesus and he backs off.

Finally, we are to take the helmet of salvation. That is we protect our mind by confidently remembering that we are saved. We don't think like we used to. **Romans 12:2 (KJV)** *2 And be not conformed to this world: but be ye transformed by the renewing of your mind, that ye may prove what is that good, and acceptable, and perfect, will of God.* The sinner became the righteous by virtue of the blood of Jesus and faith in that blood. You take hold of that truth. You are changed, completely transformed, by the truth that you know. "The Greek word is *metamorpho*. It is a complete, total change. It means ceasing to be one thing and becoming another." (Treat, p. 22) When you were born again you stopped being a sinner and became a new person with God inside; you are never the same. You changed like a caterpillar that became a butterfly, you are a new creature. The scripture above says you are changed by renewing your mind. You look at the Word of God and knowing it is true you change your thinking to line up with what God said.

Once we are fully clothed, we are to be in a continual state of prayer. Make much of your relationship. Spend time with God. I know you can't lock yourself away and pray twenty-four hours a day, but you should be so in tune with God and so comfortable approaching Him, that you are never more than a whisper away. Prayer is the natural response of the believer to every need. Be quick to call upon the Lord when you are under attack; He will send you reinforcements.

"The hosts of hell may assault you, but you meet them in that Name that once spread consternation through hell, when He put, to naught him who had the authority of death; that is the devil. [Hebrews 2:14] Satan dares not face the warrior who is clothed in Christ's righteousness, and who knows the power of that mighty Name." (Kenyon p. 64) When you come fully covered in the blood of Christ and dressed in His armor, the devil isn't sure if he is seeing the Lord or His servant. You look and act and talk like the One who won the victory and the enemy doesn't stand a chance against you.

The idea of wearing the armor of God is expressed again in the letter to the Thessalonians. **I Thessalonians 5:8 (KJV)** *8 But let us, who are of the day, be sober, putting on the breastplate of faith and love; and for an helmet, the hope of salvation.* Make sure you a dressed for success, cover yourself with the Word of God. Know who you are and stand in His victory.

I Am Who God Says I Am

John 14:12-14 (KJV) *12 Verily, verily, I say unto you, He that believeth on me, the works that I do shall he do also; and greater works than these shall he do; because I go unto my Father. 13 And whatsoever ye shall ask in my name, that will I do, that the Father may be glorified in the Son. 14 If ye shall ask any thing in my name, I will do it.*

Use the Name

There is power held within the name of Jesus for every born again believer. The authority in any name comes from one of three ways. It can be received by inheritance; the power of the father is bestowed upon the son. If in the early days of the United States your last name was Rockefeller, you had influence based upon the wealth and power your ancestor earned. Secondly, a name can be conferred on you, like when the Queen of England knighted singer Paul McCartney. He became Sir Paul McCartney. The third way is that you can earn a name by conquest, names like Alexander the Great and Caesar come to mind. The name of Jesus came all three ways. "First, He inherited a more excellent name than any of the angels as the First Begotten Son of God. Second, God gave Him a name above every name that at the name of Jesus every knee should bow in the three worlds. Third, by His conquest over sin, Satan, disease, death, hell, and the grave He acquired a name that is above all names." (Kenyon p. 5)

I want to just touch on the scriptures supporting the three-fold greatness of His name. **Isaiah 7:14 (KJV)** *14 Therefore the Lord himself shall give you a sign; Behold, a virgin shall conceive, and bear a son, and shall call his name Immanuel.* Isaiah said His name would be God with us or

God incarnate. As the Son of God, He received the name by inheritance. That name was given hundreds of years before He was conceived.

Then when Gabriel brought the news to the Virgin Mary, the name was also bestowed on Jesus. **Luke 1:30-35 (KJV)** *30 And the angel said unto her, Fear not, Mary: for thou hast found favour with God. 31 And, behold, thou shalt conceive in thy womb, and bring forth a son, and shalt call his name JESUS. 32 He shall be great, and shall be called the Son of the Highest: and the Lord God shall give unto him the throne of his father David: 33 And he shall reign over the house of Jacob for ever; and of his kingdom there shall be no end. 34 Then said Mary unto the angel, How shall this be, seeing I know not a man? 35 And the angel answered and said unto her, The Holy Ghost shall come upon thee, and the power of the Highest shall overshadow thee: therefore also that holy thing which shall be born of thee shall be called the Son of God.* The angel spoke similarly to Joseph. **Matthew 1:21 (NIV)** *21 She will give birth to a son, and you are to give him the name Jesus, because he will save his people from their sins.* Jesus is the Greek form of Joshua which means the Lord saves. So we see that twice the name was bestowed upon Jesus. And finally there was the defeat of Satan in which Jesus solidified His permanent place of authority.

First, look at the recorded victory of Christ over all our enemies. **Colossians 2:15 (KJV)** *15 And having spoiled principalities and powers, he made a shew of them openly, triumphing over them in it.* And also in the letter to the Philippians we see the name conferred on the conquering Christ. **Philippians 2:11 (KJV)** *5 Let this mind be in you, which was also in Christ Jesus: 6 Who, being in the form of God, thought it not robbery to be equal with God: 7 But made himself of no reputation, and took upon him the form* *of a servant, and was made in the likeness of men: 8 And being found in fashion as a man, he humbled himself, and became obedient unto death, even the death of the cross. 9 Wherefore God also hath highly exalted him, and given him a name which is above every name: 10 That at the name of Jesus every knee should bow, of things in heaven, and things in earth, and things under the earth; 11 And that every tongue should confess that Jesus Christ is Lord, to the glory of God the Father.* There is great power in the name of Jesus; that power was invested to benefit the church. "He has given to Him the Name that has within it the fullness of the Godhead, the wealth of the Eternities, and love of the heart of the Father-God: and, that Name is given to us. We have the right to use the Name against our enemies. We have the right to use it in our petitions. We have the right to use it in our praises and worship." (Kenyon p. 8) That name has been entrusted to us without limitations. All that Jesus ever accomplished and all He is has been invested in that name.

Only once in the gospels do we find a man who truly understood and operated in the full realm of authority. That man understood the power that a command from the Anointed One carried. **Matthew 8:5-13 (KJV)** *5 And when Jesus was entered into Capernaum, there came unto him a centurion, beseeching him, 6 And saying, Lord, my servant lieth at home sick of the palsy, grievously tormented. 7 And Jesus saith unto him, I will come and heal him. 8 The centurion answered and said, Lord, I am not worthy that thou shouldest come under my roof: but speak the word only, and my servant shall be healed. 9 For I am a man under authority, having soldiers under me: and I say to this man, Go, and he goeth; and to another, Come, and he cometh; and to my servant, Do this, and he doeth it. 10 When Jesus heard it, he marvelled, and said to them that followed, Verily I say unto you, I have not found so great faith, no, not in Israel...*

13 And Jesus said unto the centurion, Go thy way; and as thou hast believed, so be it done unto thee. And his servant was healed in the selfsame hour. That man operated in a level of faith that amazed the Lord. He simply believed that if Jesus gave the command the sickness would flee and it did. Most Christians do not understand the authority invested in the name of Jesus as well as this man did.

Jesus no longer walks the earth, but He gave us power of attorney; we have the right to use His name. **John 16:23-24 (KJV)** *23 And in that day ye shall ask me nothing. Verily, verily, I say unto you, Whatsoever ye shall ask the Father in my name, he will give it you. 24 Hitherto have ye asked nothing in my name: ask, and ye shall receive, that your joy may be full.* When we pray in the name of Jesus it is just like He asked or prayed Himself. We use His authority. He said, "In that day…" He meant in the days after the resurrection, in the day when believers were born again. That day is this day. We use His name because it is endued with all of the same power and authority that was in the man Christ Jesus when He walked the earth. "We take our privileges, and rights, in the new Covenant and pray in Jesus' name, it passes out of our hands into the hands of Jesus; He then assumes the responsibility of that prayer." (Kenyon p.4)

When my parents were first married, my mother walked into the bank and withdrew most of the money in my dad's account to pay for furniture. When asked why she thought she could do that, she told them she was his wife. They understood her to be equal owner to the account, because she now bore his name. Using another's name is the legal right of those in the relationship. The true strength and power is in what is invested in the name of the one you represent. My mother is elderly now and has Alzheimer's disease, so she is unable to manage her own finances. I was given power of attorney, which means I can legally act as if I was her. I pay her bills, and manage her bank accounts. I have the authority to cash in all of my mother's assets, and make medical decisions. I have access to all she owns; the only limitation I have is in the amount invested in her name. I could not write a check for a million dollars because that is more than is in her account. I could however write a check for every last cent and it would be cashed without hesitation. I could open a credit card based on her income and it would be granted because I have the power to use her name and she is legally bound to back it. In the same way, Jesus gave us power of attorney. We have the right to use His name to cash a check on the account of heaven. I might be able to make a request large enough to bankrupt my mother, but I could never bankrupt heaven. "When Jesus gave us the legal right to use this name, the Father knew all that the name would imply when breathed in prayer by oppressed souls, and it is His joy to recognize that name." (Kenyon p. 5) Whatever I need, Jesus is able to supply and there is more than enough invested in His name to bring it to pass.

The disciples found that they could operate in a realm that tapped into His power. **Luke 10:17 (KJV)** *17 And the seventy returned again with joy, saying, Lord, even the devils are subject unto us through thy name.* That power wasn't just for the disciples, but for all believers.

"God's power will work the same through any born-again believer as it did through Peter and John at the Gate Beautiful. Jesus gave us His Name and the authority to use it in Mark 16." (Dufresne p. 27) **Mark 16:15-18 (KJV)** 15 *And he said unto them, Go ye into all the world, and preach the gospel to every creature. 16 He that believeth and is baptized shall be saved; but he that believeth not shall be damned. 17*

And these signs shall follow them that believe; (Notice is does not say signs would follow the apostles or ministers, or the early disciples. It said the ones who believe. I believe, so I can expect the power invested in that name to work for me.) *In my name shall they cast out devils; they shall speak with new tongues; 18 They shall take up serpents; and if they drink any deadly thing, it shall not hurt them; they shall lay hands on the sick, and they shall recover.* Jesus gave us the right to use His name. "They made a discovery—the Name of the Man whom they had loved, whom they had seen nailed to that cross in nakedness, now has power equal to the power that He, Himself exercised when He was among them." (Kenyon p. 22) When the name of Jesus was spoken in faith, it produced powerful results.

Miraculously, Jesus gave us full authority and full access to all He possesses and all He controls. Think about that, He who has a limitless supply gave us power of attorney. How amazing that we have access to the resources of heaven. There is great power in the name of Jesus and we have the legal right to use it.

It was the power invested in the name of Jesus that Peter used when he healed the lame man in the early days of the church. This man had been laying at the gate every time Jesus and His disciples walked by. **Acts 3:6 (KJV)** *6 Then Peter said, Silver and gold have I none; but such as I have give I thee: In the name of Jesus Christ of Nazareth rise up and walk.* Peter used the name of Jesus and a miracle occurred. He wrote a check on God's account, signed it with the name of Jesus and withdrew a miracle from the resources of heaven. Jesus had already established healing in His own ministry and told the disciples that they were to do as He did.

John 14:12-14 (KJV) *12 Verily, verily, I say unto you, He that believeth on me, the works that I do shall he do also; and greater works than these shall he do; because I go unto my Father. 13 And whatsoever ye shall ask in my name, that will I do, that the Father may be glorified in the Son. 14 If ye shall ask any thing in my name, I will do it.* The word 'ask' here is not a request, it is a demand; it is made based on the work of Christ. You step out in faith and demand your rights based on the covenant relationship you have with God as a believer. You use the authority invested in the name of Jesus and circumstances change. "As long as Satan can keep you in unbelief or hold you in the arena of reason, he'll whip you in every battle. But if you'll hold him in the arena of faith and the Spirit, you'll whip him every time. He won't argue with you about the Name of Jesus—he's afraid of that Name." (Hagin p. 22) That is exactly what Peter did when the lame man was healed at the Beautiful Gate. He believed the person of Jesus was present in the name, and that the anointing would do the work demanded in that name.

Armed with a confidence that Jesus was present in them and would back their words, the disciples boldly ministered. Let's look at the miracle in a little more detail. **Acts 3:1-6 (KJV)** *1 Now Peter and John went up together into the temple at the hour of prayer, being the ninth hour. 2 And a certain man lame from his mother's womb was carried, whom they laid daily at the gate of the temple which is called Beautiful, to ask alms of them that entered into the temple; 3 Who seeing Peter and John about to go into the temple asked an alms. 4 And Peter, fastening his eyes upon him with John, said, Look on us. 5 And he gave heed unto them, expecting to receive something of them. 6 Then Peter said, Silver and gold have I none; but such as I have give I thee: In the name of Jesus Christ of Nazareth rise up and walk.* They said they were not giving him money, but they possessed something else and could give it. What they had was the same spirit that raised Christ from the dead. They had the same power that had lifted others from a bed of affliction. They had the right to use the name of Jesus to make a demand on the anointing for healing. They used the name with authority. They did not whisper it, but loudly commanded the man to be healed and grabbed him by the hand and dragged him into a standing position. They were confident. Peter and John were using their faith in the blood of Jesus and the power invested in His name to get results for the lame man.

Acts 3:7-8 (KJV) *7 And he took him by the right hand, and lifted him up: and immediately his feet and ankle bones received strength. 8 And he leaping up stood, and walked, and entered with them into the temple, walking, and leaping, and praising God.* That day was his day to receive and he did. Peter did not pray. He commanded his body to be healed by the authority invested in the name of Jesus. The results were undeniable, the man had his legs and feet completely healed and he gave glory to God.

The disciples used their confidence in the testimony of Christ and what was conferred upon the name of Jesus to accomplish the same things they knew He would do on the earth. You and I are included in that confident group of believers when we use the name with authority.

These two disciples pleased and glorified God by using their spiritual authority to get the lame man healed. They did not pray and ask if it was God's will for him to be healed. They exercised their right to continue the ministry of Jesus. "For the first time, we come in vital contact with this strange power vested in the Name of Jesus. This miracle created a sensation; the disciples were arrested, put in jail until the morrow. Through this miracle the number of disciples had increased to about five thousand." (Kenyon p. 39) They purposefully used the name of Jesus, trusting in all He did on the cross; they were co-workers with Christ. They acted as they had seen Jesus act and they assumed He was present to back their words as they called for this man to be miraculously healed.

When questioned concerning the miracle this was Peter's bold reply. **Acts 3:12-16 (KJV)** *12 And when Peter saw it, he answered unto the people, Ye men of Israel, why marvel ye at this? or why look ye so earnestly on us, as though by our own power or holiness we had made this man to walk? 13 The God of Abraham, and of Isaac, and of Jacob, the God of our fathers, hath glorified His Son Jesus; whom ye delivered up, and denied him in the presence of Pilate, when he was determined to let him go. 14 But ye denied the Holy One and the Just, and desired a murderer to be granted unto you; 15 And killed the Prince of life, whom God hath raised from the dead; whereof we are witnesses. 16 <u>And his name through faith in his name hath made this man strong</u>, whom ye see and know: yea, the faith which is by him hath given him this perfect soundness in the presence of you all.* They did not say that they were Christ's Apostles; they did not say they were preachers or members of a church. They did not say they had a special gifting. What they said was, Jesus, the Son of God, was the healer and their access to healing was through faith in His name. "We have a four-fold right to use the Name. First, we are born into the family of God and the Name belongs to the family. Second, we are baptized in the Name and being baptized into the Name, we are baptized into Christ Himself. Third, it was conferred upon us by Jesus who gave us the power of attorney. Fourth, we are commissioned as ambassadors to go and herald this

Name among the nations." (Kenyon p. 26) We are to carry out His ministry using His power and the authority invested in the body of Christ through His name.

Even the Sanhedrin recognized that there was power in the name of Jesus and they forbid the disciples to use the name. **Acts 4:17-20 (KJV)** *17 But that it spread no further among the people, let us straitly threaten them, that they speak henceforth to no man in this name. 18 And they called them, and commanded them not to speak at all nor teach in the name of Jesus. 19 But Peter and John answered and said unto them, Whether it be right in the sight of God to hearken unto you more than unto God, judge ye. 20 For we cannot but speak the things which we have seen and heard.* They did not fear those threats but instead asked for more boldness to further the cause of Christ and the use of His name. **Acts 4:29-31 (KJV)** *29 And now, Lord, behold their threatenings: and grant unto thy servants, that with all boldness they may speak thy word, 30 By stretching forth thine hand to heal; and that signs and wonders may be done by the name of thy holy child Jesus. 31 And when they had prayed, the place was shaken where they were assembled together; and they were all filled with the Holy Ghost, and they spake the word of God with boldness.* The church was alive with the revelation of the authority to use His name. Believers who know who they are and act upon what they know are dangerous to the devil and his minions. **Acts 5:27-32 (KJV)** *27 And when they had brought them, they set them before the council: and the high priest asked them, 28 Saying, Did not we straitly command you that ye should not teach in this name? and, behold, ye have filled Jerusalem with your doctrine, and intend to bring this man's blood upon us. 29 Then Peter and the other apostles answered and said, We ought to obey God rather than men. 30 The God of our fathers raised up Jesus,* *whom ye slew and hanged on a tree. 31 Him hath God exalted with his right hand to be a Prince and a Saviour, for to give repentance to Israel, and forgiveness of sins. 32 And we are his witnesses of these things; and so is also the Holy Ghost, whom God hath given to them that obey him.* Walking in the powerful relationship they had with Jesus made them both bold and unstoppable.

When God saved and called Saul of Tarsus, the thing that God said concerning him was that he would carry the name. **Acts 9:15 (KJV)** *15 But the Lord said unto him, Go thy way: for he is a chosen vessel unto me, to bear my name before the Gentiles, and kings, and the children of Israel:*

The first time God showed me that He was calling me to preach, He said almost those same words to me. I was in a church service and there was a powerful anointing. I was seated on the stage as part of the worship team. The Lord told me to stand so I stood, and as soon as I obeyed, I could see in the spirit. In the spirit my hands were cupped and I was staring into them trying to see what it was I carried there. I knew that what was in my hands was very important. Finally, the Lord said, "The name, the name, the name, My Word." For the past 38 years I have been proclaiming His Word and trying to faithfully carry that name endued with the power it contains.

That power is firmly attached to our blood bought right to use the name of Jesus. **Mark 16:15 (KJV)** *15 And he said unto them, Go ye into all the world, and preach the gospel to every creature.* The early disciples did just that. **Mark 16:20 (KJV)** *20 And they went forth, and preached everywhere, the Lord working with them, and confirming the word with signs following. Amen.* None of that great commission has lessened over time. We still have the mission to minister to both Christians and unbelievers. We are fully equipped to represent Jesus as He was and is. We are more than able to bring healing to the sick, salvation to the lost and deliverance to all who are oppressed through His name. **I Corinthians 1:9 (KJV)** *9 God is faithful, by whom ye were called unto the fellowship of his Son Jesus Christ our Lord.* You have the right and even the responsibility to use the name of Jesus.

The early church knew the power invested in the name of Jesus. They boldly proclaimed Him Lord and Healer. Some people seem to be afraid to use the name of Jesus to get what they need. They are afraid it will not work for them. That name has not lost any of its power, but some of the church has lost confidence in it. Jesus told us to ask, to use His authority and to expect good things. **Matthew 7:7-11 (KJV)** *7 Ask, and it shall be given you; seek, and ye shall find; knock, and it shall be opened unto you: 8 For every one that asketh receiveth; and he that seeketh findeth; and to him that knocketh it shall be opened. 9 Or what man is there of you, whom if his son ask bread, will he give him a stone? 10 Or if he ask a fish, will he give him a serpent? 11 If ye then, being evil, know how to give good gifts unto your children, how much more shall your Father which is in heaven give good things to them that ask him?* He said ask, and keep on asking. He said we can trust that whatever good we ask of our Father in heaven, we can expect to receive. "From the cradle with its prophecy, to the cross with its tragedy, and sweeping down through the ages, that Name has steadily grown until today, the Jew, the Gentile, and heathen of all lands are compelled to recognize that Name." (Kenyon p. 46)

I John 3:23 (KJV) *23 And this is his commandment, That we should believe on the name of his Son Jesus Christ, and love one another, as he gave us commandment.* The early believers just believed the name would bring His presence and do what needed to be done. Since we are the saved, having believed on the name to receive the benefits of the cross, we can now believe in that same power invested in His name. The Word of God and the Name of God who became flesh will back what we demand be done by the use of that wonderful name. "The command that we should believe in the Name is literally that we should believe the Name—the preposition 'in' is not in the Greek. That we should believe the Name—believe it for what it stands—believe it for all it means in the heart of the Father—that we believe the Name." (Kenyon p.48) We can take our blood bought authority, full of His invisible power, and minister it to others through the name of Jesus.

When we pray, the words "in the name of Jesus" flow readily from our lips, but they are not some magic incantation. They are you declaring that your entire confidence for an answer is based on what He has done at the cross. We are using His name to assure the answer. If we really trust in what is behind the name of Jesus we will have boldness to pray and receive.

You are born again through the power invested in that name and you are an authorized user of that same name to do the whole of the ministry delegated to believers. Use the name of Jesus with confidence, because it belongs to you.

Matthew 12:37 (KJV) *37 For by thy words thou shalt be justified, and by thy words thou shalt be condemned.*

What Did You Say

So many of us as believers are trying to stand in faith and operate according to the Word of God. The problem is our big mouth. We do not take control of what we say and we think it won't matter, but it does. **James 1:26 (KJV)** *26 If any man among you seem to be religious, and bridleth not his tongue, but deceiveth his own heart, this man's religion is vain.* The Lord told us our words matter. **Matthew 12:34-37 (KJV)** *...for out of the abundance of the heart the mouth speaketh. 35 A good man out of the good treasure of the heart bringeth forth good things: and an evil man out of the evil treasure bringeth forth evil things. 36 But I say unto you, That every idle word that men shall speak, they shall give account thereof in the day of judgment. 37 For by thy words thou shalt be justified, and by thy words thou shalt be condemned.* Words are powerful; they have creative or destructive ability inside them. We win or lose based upon what we believe and what we say.

The Bible was always meant to be both believed and spoken. In Joshua we read **Joshua 1:8 (KJV)** *8 This book of the law shall not depart out of thy mouth; but thou shalt meditate therein day and night, that thou mayest observe to do according to all that is written therein: for then thou shalt make thy way prosperous, and then thou shalt have good* *success.* That Hebrew word translated as meditate was ***Haga*** and in this verse meditating on the Word of God means to ponder and to mutter or speak it to yourself or to others. We are to be speaking the scriptures over our needs. "God's Word that is conceived in your heart, then formed on the tongue, and spoken out of your mouth, becomes a spiritual force releasing the ability of God within you." (Capps 2, p.7) If indeed our words have such power, we should choose them wisely. It is in our best interest to speak what the Word of God says and to align our conversation with the purposes and plans of God and to speak our desired outcome.

Words are eternal. Once a word is spoken it continues to travel out into the atmosphere. Scientists can verify that sounds from many light years away are still moving through space. God's spoken Words are still at work.

God has invested heavily in the spoken Word. He used His words to create and has invested in the earth by sending Jesus who was the Word made flesh. **John 1:1-4 (KJV)** *1 In the beginning was the Word, and the Word was with God, and the Word was God. 2 The same was in the beginning with God. 3 All things were made by him; and without him was not anything made that was made. 4 In him was life; and the life was the light of men.* Everything that was ever created was in essence a thought in the heart of God that took shape by being spoken into the atmosphere. The very Word of God came forth and ministered unto men in a way they could understand and showed them the power of God expressed.

Hebrews 1:1-3 (KJV) *1 God, who at sundry times and in divers manners spake in time past unto the fathers by the prophets, 2 Hath in these last days spoken unto us by his Son, whom he hath appointed heir of all things, by whom* *also he made the worlds; 3 Who being the brightness of his glory, and the express image of his person, and upholding all things by the word of his power, when he had by himself purged our sins, sat down on the right hand of the Majesty on high;* Jesus was truth personified; He was the express will of the Father and every word He spoke lined up with the heart of His father. "The Word was God...upholding all things by the word of His power. God released His ability in Word form and it upholds all things. The whole universe stands in obedience to His Words. God's ability is in His Word. We must learn to release that ability within us by rightly dividing His Words." (Capps p. 10)

God created men in His image. He made us like Him. God did all of His creating with the Words He spoke. He made you a speaking spirit. That is He gave you the right to use your voice like He used His, to change circumstances. Every word you speak has some effect on you and those around you. Those words can change circumstances. While the whole of the spirit world is under the control of God's Word, the natural world is to be controlled by men speaking faith filled words—His Word. Any time we use scripture it is God still speaking in the earth. Some of those faith filled words are released in prayer. "Effective prayer will destroy the kingdom of darkness and release the ability of God in the earth. As the Church of Jesus Christ comes to the knowledge of its authority in prayer as a joint-heir with Christ, it will partake of His divine nature. Then shall the Church proclaim boldly, It is Written!" (Capps p. 15)

Hebrews 11: 3 (KJV) *3 Through faith we understand that the worlds were framed by the word of God, so that things which are seen were not made of things which do appear.* "The world was not made out of things you can see. You can't see spoken words nor can you see faith with the physical eye. The words that God spoke out of His mouth framed this universe set it in motion and it stands today in obedience to the Words God spoke." (Capps 2 p. 13) God said let there be light and light was. We know that command is still at work because darkness has never overcome the light.

"Prayer gets its power from faith, and faith works by love. Somehow down through the years we have gotten the idea that prayer makes faith work. It doesn't. Faith makes prayer work. Faith will work without prayer, but prayer will not work without faith." (Capps p. 34) Prayer is effective when we learn the will of God through reading His Word, and then we line up with what He has said. If we pray what He said we will get good results. "Sometimes we pray just trying to muster up some faith. That is not scriptural. Faith comes by hearing the Word of God, not by praying. Go to the Word of God and hear the Word until faith comes; don't be too quick to pray." (Capps p. 47) Get a solid Biblical foundation and then stand upon it in prayer.

Romans 10:17 (KJV) *17 So then faith cometh by hearing, and hearing by the word of God.* Notice that it does not say it comes by reading or by having read or having heard in the past. Hearing is present tense; it is now. "The Greek says, *"Faith cometh by report and the report by the declaration of God."* So we know that faith comes by hearing the ***rhema,*** the spoken Word of God. When we hear ourselves speaking, saying what God said, it will produce faith in us more quickly than if we hear someone else saying it. Hearing your own voice speak God's Word will excite your heart to action." (Capps p. 92) What you say on a continual basis you will eventually believe. And whatever we really believe we can ask for in prayer and receive. When the Bible comes out of my mouth, it is as if God was again speaking...my words are the voice of God's Word. That establishes it in heaven and on earth.

Faith like God's will speak. **Mark 11:22-24 (KJV)** *22 And Jesus answering saith unto them, Have faith in God. 23 For verily I say unto you, That whosoever shall say unto this mountain, Be thou removed, and be thou cast into the sea; and shall not doubt in his heart, but shall believe that those things which he saith shall come to pass; he shall have whatsoever he saith. 24 Therefore I say unto you, What things soever ye desire, when ye pray, believe that ye receive them, and ye shall have them.* He used the word say or saith four times, He said faith once and believe twice. Evidently the speaking part matters. When you believe you pray and in praying you say it, then you keep on agreeing with the words you have already spoken and it will happen. Not everything we pray for happens instantaneously; I wish it did. Most of the time, the words we say, the things we pray, work like seeds. You plant your faith seed by speaking and then you leave it in the ground to grow. You do nothing that will harm your seed. You do not dig it up to see if it is germinating; you let it grow. The scriptures tell us something about this. **Genesis 8:22 (KJV)** *22 While the earth remaineth, seedtime and harvest, and cold and heat, and summer and winter, and day and night shall not cease.* I like to think of it like this; seed is planted, then we allow time for it to grow, and over the long run, a harvest is guaranteed. Faith produces in a process as natural as the crops the early readers planted.

Our words need to line up with His Word. His Word contains within it all that is needed to produce. We get that Word firmly established in our hearts. **Proverbs 4:23 (KJV)** *23 Keep thy heart with all diligence; for out of it are the issues of life.* When the Word of God reigns in the heart it can become a powerful force. It changes how we think and then how we speak. **Proverbs 23:7 (KJV)** *7 For as he thinketh in his heart, so is he:* The promises of God deeply believed will establish us in faith. It is a perfect seed. We plant it with our mouth, speaking in line with what He has already established and it will grow strong. **Hebrews 4:12-16 (KJV)** *12 For the word of God is quick, and powerful, and sharper than any two-edged sword, piercing even to the dividing asunder of soul and spirit, and of the joints and marrow, and is a discerner of the thoughts and intents of the heart. 13 Neither is there any creature that is not manifest in his sight: but all things are naked and opened unto the eyes of him with whom we have to do. 14 Seeing then that we have a great high priest, that is passed into the heavens, Jesus the Son of God, let us hold fast our profession.* We keep the words of our mouth continually speaking a confession of faith in God and in His promises. *16 Let us therefore come boldly unto the throne of grace, that we may obtain mercy, and find grace to help in time of need.* This text has within it a powerful truth. God's Word spoken from the lips of the believer is powerful and mighty. Ephesians 6:17 calls the Word of God a sword. Your Bible on the nightstand is not powerful until you take those Words inside of you and act as if they are true. If you really believe it, you will say it. "The spoken Word of God is the Sword of the Spirit. We call the Bible our sword, but it is not really the sword. It may be the substance the sword is made of, but it is not sword until it proceeds out of your mouth." (Capps p. 152) That Word is not any less powerful than it was when God first spoke it.

John 15:7 (KJV) *7 If ye abide in me, and my words abide in you, ye shall ask what ye will, and it shall be done unto you.* If His words are living in you because you are His child, you can ask anything. You can ask it because your heart and His are the same. **Luke 6:45 (KJV)** *45 A good man out of the good treasure of his heart bringeth* *forth that which is good; and an evil man out of the evil treasure of his heart bringeth forth that which is evil: for of the abundance of the heart his mouth speaketh.* What fills your heart comes out of your mouth. Some people have no filter and so whatever pops into their head just comes out of their mouth. His Word becomes your word by association. The more time you spend with the Lord and the more you read the Bible, the more you will be speaking His Word. The one who is really saved and in love with the Lord will learn His Word and it will come out in daily conversation.

Some people have a misconception about what prayer is. They need to realize that everything we say in prayer should line up with His revealed will. It is not good form to pray about how bad things are and how mistreated or sick you are. That is not praying in faith it is just whining. Complaining to God is not the same thing as praying. Do not go to God and just tell Him your problems. God knows your problems. Go to Him in faith and speak the desired answer to your prayer. Get His Word on the topic and then speak the Word back to the One who wrote it. That will work. **Isaiah 1: 18 (KJV)** *18 Come now, and let us reason together, saith the LORD: though your sins be as scarlet, they shall be as white as snow; though they be red like crimson, they shall be as wool.* God wants us to bring His Words to remembrance. He wants us to present our case.

Jeremiah 1:12 (KJV) *12 Then said the LORD unto me...for I will hasten my word to perform it.* The Amplified Bible says He is active and alert watching over His words. God is ready to do what He has said when it comes out of your mouth. He wants to do what He has promised us. **Hebrews 3:1 (KJV)** *1 Wherefore, holy brethren, partakers of the heavenly calling, consider the Apostle and High Priest of our profession, Christ Jesus;* Your profession is the whole of the words you speak. Maybe it would be more accurate to say it is your confession. That doesn't only mean while you are praying. It is what you say on a daily basis. Jesus is our lawyer, our advocate, our High Priest, and He watches over the words we say. "When I pray speaking faith-filled words concerning the things I desire, I can see Jesus, seated at the right hand of God the Father, nudging the Father and saying, 'He is holding fast to the Word, saying the same things You said; He is returning your Word to You. Now let's perform it just the way he said it.' Jesus confesses to the Father what I say if it agrees with the Word of God." (Capps p. 94) Your words either build your faith in the problem or the solution.

Jesus did not talk about problems, but He did speak to the problem. When the storms came, He did not ask the Father to stop the storm. He spoke to the wind and the sea, "Peace be still" and the storm obeyed Him. When Jesus encountered a man with a demon spirit, He spoke to the spirit, "Come out of him" and it did. He gave us an example of how to deal with problems.

When you go to God with His Word and then release the problem to Him, He can finish the work. When Bob was a young man, he inherited a pocket watch from his grandfather. It was precious to him because he knew that his grandfather had carried it every day of his adult life. When Bob was a little boy and sat upon his grandfather's knee listening to the stories he told. Bob had held that watch in his hands and listened to his grandfather talk. Those memories made the watch priceless to Bob. It was also quite valuable in and of itself. It was fine craftsmanship and it was an antique. The only problem was that it no longer kept time. The young man went to a jeweler and asked about repairing the watch. They talked for some time and the whole time they spoke Bob held on to the watch. Finally, he said, "When do you think you can get it working?" The jeweler looked at him and smiled, then he said, "Not until it is in my hands; you will have to trust me with it to get it repaired." That is the way we act, we want God to take care of our problem but we hold on to it. No, give it to God and then He who is the master craftsman can take care of it.

Sometimes if we cannot speak in faith, we might want to just say nothing. Kenneth Hagin once said, "You can have doubt in your head but it won't go to your heart unless you let it out of your mouth." **Proverbs 13:1-3 (KJV)** *1 A wise son heareth his father's instruction: but a scorner heareth not rebuke. 2 A man shall eat good by the fruit of his mouth: but the soul of the transgressors shall eat violence. 3 He that keepeth his mouth keepeth his life: but he that openeth wide his lips shall have destruction.* Philips, Craig & Dean have a song we might want to learn. They entitled it *Let My Words Be Few.* Since He is God, and we are not, we would do well to spend more time listening and less time talking until we know what the Lord has said; It is always wise to repeat scripture. "Words work. They will work for you, just as they worked for Jesus. They work for you or against you, whether you realize it or not." (Capps 2 p. 90) We can have what we say, so we dare not confess sickness and poverty and failure. "Active faith in the Word brings God on the scene. Fear brings Satan on the scene." (Capps 2 p. 92) **Proverbs 18:21 (KJV)** *21 Death and life are in the power of the tongue: and they that love it shall eat the fruit thereof.* We have been given the right and delegated the authority to use words to shape our environment. We must choose them wisely.

Romans 5:17 (KJV) *17 For if by one man's offence death reigned by one; much more they which receive abundance of grace and of the gift of righteousness shall reign in life by one, Jesus Christ.*

Sharing His Victory

Jesus taught that the only way to take Satan down was for a stronger one to come and forcefully take whatever he held captive. **Mark 3:26-27 (KJV)** *26 And if Satan rise up against himself, and be divided, he cannot stand, but hath an end. 27 No man can enter into a strong man's house, and spoil his goods, except he will first bind the strong man; and then he will spoil his house.* "The strong man is Satan who carefully protects his possessions, the dominion and authority which he subliminally captured from Adam without any fear of counterattack. Jesus, however, is the stronger one, who comes to legally overpower him, and dispossess his most prized holdings, and ultimately restores the same authority back to man who lost it in the beginning." (Trombley p. 28) **I John 3:8 (KJV)** *8 He that committeth sin is of the devil; for the devil sinneth from the beginning. For this purpose the Son of God was manifested, that he might destroy the works of the devil.*

Jesus did that for us. He came stronger than death. Stronger than Adam's sin and defeated the devil. He went into the darkest places and brought in the light. He found all that Adam gave up that day in the garden and He brought it back into a place where we could stand in victory once more. "All that He earned in this colossal conquest He unselfishly shared with the former captives. This act brings us to the zenith of redemption, the seating of Christ Jesus as our legal representative before and beside the Father. A new man, immortal, incorruptible, never again subject to death, is now my Advocate in heaven." (Trombley p. 106)

Jesus told us earlier that He had all authority. If He has it, the devil does not. For a season, the devil held mankind captive; he dominated and manipulated them. But he has no right to do so now. Jesus went to the cross, took the power of death away from him and regained the title deed to planet earth.

Paul said his deep desire is that we would know who we are through that victory. It is the will of God that all Jesus purchased for us legally, becomes our experientially. That is not only that we are free by the demands of justice having been met but that we apply it and recognize what Jesus is actually doing in us. Paul prayed that we would see the fact that we are already seated with Christ and nothing that the devil tries to do has any power over us. **[Ephesians 1:17-23]** Jesus put an end to Satan's attempt at worldwide domination. He set us free and then He made us co-victors. You may feel like a loser but you are a winner legally.

Jesus, the perfect Son of God, came to this fallen world. He came as one of us. He was born in poverty; He took His first breath in a stable. He worked among men and taught and preached and did the miraculous. Then the devil, who could find no fault or weakness in Him, drove men to crucify Jesus. On that cross the devil was defeated. Sin and death died there. Shame and sorrow and sickness and depression were buried in the tomb with Jesus. When Jesus came out alive, the glorious conqueror, so did we. The whole time He walked this earth, the whole time He suffered and lay in that grave, we were in Him. He carried us in His heart. He became our substitute and when it was all over, He seated us with Him in heavenly places. We joined Jesus there on His royal throne. All that had weighed us down was lifted off of us. Now every evil thing is under His feet by conquest and under our feet by His decree. When Jesus won, we won.

We are so united with Jesus that He called us His own body. The feet are in the body and all things are under His feet. Paul wrote to the believers in Rome. **Romans 16:20 (KJV)** *20 And the God of peace shall bruise Satan under your feet shortly.* It doesn't say under Christ's feet but under yours because He passed the baton to us, this is our part of the race. "The feet, being members of His body, will be used by the Lord to fully subdue His enemies…God is committed to ruling the universe through the church. It is through the church that all satanic opposition must be put down. He has willed that through the church He will exercise His Lordship." (Trombley p. 107)

In the Spirit world, we were there. When Jesus suffered and died, so did we. When He rose from the dead in victory, so did we. When He sat down in the place of authority, so did we. We are one with Him. **Ephesians 2:1 (KJV)** *1 And you hath he quickened, who were dead in trespasses and sins;* Quickened means made alive. We are more alive than we have ever been. We have spiritual life. When Adam was first created, he had the breath of God inside him. He was so alive that there was no death at all. When he sinned, openly rebelling against the Father, that life went out. That life is back and it is ours. When we were born again, life flooded our being.

Ephesians 2:4-10 (KJV) *4 But God, who is rich in mercy, for his great love wherewith he loved us, 5 Even when we were dead in sins, hath quickened us together with Christ, (by grace ye are saved;) 6 And hath raised us up together, and made us sit together in heavenly places in Christ Jesus: 7 That in the ages to come he might shew the exceeding riches of his grace in his kindness toward us through Christ Jesus. 8 For by grace are ye saved through faith; and that not of yourselves: it is the gift of God: 9 Not of works, lest any man should boast. 10 For we are his workmanship, created in Christ Jesus unto good works, which God hath before ordained that we should walk in them.*

We stand or fall according to whose side we are on. If we are not actively on God's side, standing in what Christ has done the enemy will see our inactivity and try to reclaim ground already won by the Lord. That first Adam failed but Jesus, the last Adam, succeeded and brought life back to the whole of Adam's race. Everyone who is willing can come out of bondage. Every believer is free. "Through the new birth, we are now part of His body, as we have borne the image of the first Adam we must also bear the image of the last Adam. Everything Jesus was while He walked on the earth as a man was exactly what Adam could have been, had he not thrown it all away. Everything our magnificent Christ was and is, is exactly what we are and will ever be." (Trombley p. 109)

We have been set free, not just to survive, but to rule and reign in life. We can see it when we recognize the extent of our unity with Jesus. "In vital union with Him, when He tasted death and subdued the powers of darkness, disarming and paralyzing them, we were participators in His victory. When He violently snatched the keys of death and hell from Satan, released the captives, and removed Paradise from Hades to Heaven, we were in Him and shared that victory. When He ascended on high and took His rightful place beside the Father, we shared His exaltation with Him. When the Father said, 'Rule until all your enemies become your footstool, until Satan and his government of rebels are under your feet,' we were included in Him." (Trombley p. 109)

That place of victory is a legal position. It has been authenticated by the Word. Since that is the case, we access it by faith. We believe that what Jesus did for us and purchased for us is ours now. It belongs to us. We act upon what He did. We make it ours by believing it in our hearts and saying it openly. It is already truth, so we can declare it to be ours. **Romans 5:17 (KJV)** *17 For if by one man's offence death reigned by one; much more they which receive abundance of grace and of the gift of righteousness shall reign in life by one, Jesus Christ.* Notice that verse does not say we just barely get by in life. It says we reign; we rule. We are powerful and in charge and triumphant though His victory. We have dominion in this world. We have to force out the previous tenant. The devil has pushed us around long enough. That bully has been soundly defeated and now we are free. "As a Christian you must first of all 'see' your promises and then fight for them. Your liberation from Satan's kingdom is effective only to the degree you lay hold of it by faith." (Trombley p. 112) The devil will try to discourage you. He will lie to you and tell you that you are nothing. He is trying to steal your identity, he wants you to doubt that you are saved and free and one with God. He wants you to forget that you are the one with authority to rule and reign. That bully wants you walking in fear and unbelief again, but you are not who he says you are. You are who God says you are and there is a world of difference.

Jesus took the symbol of authority away from the devil. The one with the keys has the authority. When I go to the church, if it happens to be locked it is not a barrier to me, because I have the key. I am authorized to come and go as I like. The one with the key has special access. Satan used to have the keys of death but not any longer. Jesus stripped the devil of the keys and the rights and authority he had on the earth and now that power and authority has been given unto the believer. **Revelation 1:18 (KJV)** *18 I am he that liveth, and was dead; and, behold, I am alive for evermore, Amen; and have the keys of hell and of death.* Not only does He have them, but He shares them with you. **Matthew 16:19 (KJV)** *19 And I will give unto thee the keys of the kingdom of heaven: and whatsoever thou shalt bind on earth shall be bound in heaven: and whatsoever thou shalt loose on earth shall be loosed in heaven.* This Word authorizes both the church and the individual to act in His stead. When we use His name it is as if Jesus spoke the words.

Once you are saved, the devil is powerless in your life. He only reigns where you allow him to by not asserting your rights and authority as a believer. Jesus has already told us how to handle the attack of the devil. "You use the authority I've already conferred upon you to resist him. My grace has sufficiently overpowered him with the Word in order that you can use that same Word, which is the power of God unto salvation." (Trombley p. 117) **Revelation 12:10-11 (KJV)** *10 And I heard a loud voice saying in heaven, Now is come salvation, and strength, and the kingdom of our God, and the power of his Christ: for the accuser of our brethren is cast down, which accused them before our God day and night. 11 And they overcame him by the blood of the Lamb, and by the word of their testimony; and they loved not their lives unto the death.* Every believer who will ever face adversity can win against that defeated devil by trusting in their identification with Jesus Christ and His identification with us. God fully committed Himself to mankind. We are in vital union with the One who rules the universe. We must remember that. We are the blood bought children of God, born again into His family, and we say so. Our confession of who we are in Christ makes us victorious. We overcome every obstacle and all the attempts to destroy us by continually trusting that we are blood bought and by saying with our own mouth what God has already spoken over us.

You might fail sometimes. You will not sail through this life without ever encountering the enemy. He will try to discourage you. He will try to make you sin and then turn around and make you feel guilty about it. Remember these two scriptures. **John 16:33 (KJV)** *33 These things I have spoken unto you, that in me ye might have peace. In the world ye shall have tribulation: but be of good cheer; I have overcome the world.* If we struggle, we simply do what He has told us to do. **I John 1:9 (KJV)** *9 If we confess our sins, he is faithful and just to forgive us our sins, and to cleanse us from all unrighteousness.* My victory is tied to His; it is in the cross of Christ. I overcome one day at a time. I walk out His victory, and if I mess up, I go back to the blood and receive the forgiveness He already paid for and I move on to my next battle. I am assured of the victory as long as I stay close to the One who seated me in His own seat of authority.

Hebrews 11:1 (KJV) *1 Now faith is the substance of things hoped for, the evidence of things not seen.*

Walking by Faith

There is little that we can achieve in life until we start walking by faith. "We are born into eternal life through faith; we are declared righteous before God by faith; we are forgiven by faith; we are healed by faith; we understand the mysteries of creation by faith; we learn God's Word by faith; by faith we understand things to come; we walk by faith and not by sight; we overcome the world by faith; we enter God's rest by faith; and we are controlled and empowered by the Holy Spirit by faith." (Lindsey p. 21) We stand or fall based on what we believe. It is not based on what we once believed, but on what we continue to believe. We must walk by faith daily.

Not everything we need in life comes to us on a silver platter. God responds to faith, which is a confident assurance that He has provided all that we need through Jesus. Faith takes hold of what was already in the blood and was promised in the Word and does not let go. Faith activates the power of God. If I want something, I have to believe it is mine; I take it now. Most of what is already ours in Christ has to be fought for or at least claimed by faith. Our foundation for all we believe is the Bible. **Hebrews 11:1 (AMP)** *Now faith is the assurance (the confirmation, the title-deed) of the things [we] hope for, being the proof of the things [we] do* *not see and the conviction of their reality—faith perceiving as real fact what is not revealed to the senses.* Faith says that I have what I prayed for now. My senses may not agree, but the spirit man inside me knows that I have what I believe. I can only receive what I know is mine. I believe what God says. So I look to the Scripture and I see what God said and I cling to it with all I have until it manifests in the natural world. You can never live in the past or the future, so take the present and live in the now. Believe in the now. Establish the Bible as the standard of truth in the now. Let the truth rule in you, in spite of your circumstances. The Word of God does not change and it has not lost its power.

Faith is the source of our strength and provision. There is no other force that can match faith or replace it. Real faith will never let go. Faith does not waver. It does not sit down and take a break. Find scripture to support your request and then hold fast to that promise. Stand and stand and stand upon the Word of God; eventually, your faith will make such headway that your situation will line up with the redemption in Christ Jesus, and you will receive.

"The Bible teaches that the power of faith is in its object, not in faith itself, much less in our imagination. Our positive attitude should come from Christ-confidence instead of humanly produced self-confidence. Paul gave our correct model in Philippians." (Lindsey p. 14) **Philippians 4:13 (KJV)** *13 I can do all things through Christ which strengtheneth me.* I can do very little in and of myself, but when I look to Him, and trust in Him, nothing is impossible. **II Corinthians 12: 9 (KJV)** *9 And he said unto me, My grace is sufficient for thee: for my strength is made perfect in weakness.* God's grace is more than enough to get us through anything. His grace can never be a rejection of your need, but is rather a way through it. When we let go of the problem and release it into God's hands, He is free to do what we could not. God delights in using someone the world thinks of as weak—a nobody. He took three murderers named Moses, David, and Paul to become great leaders. He took Peter who denied he even knew Jesus, and used him to shepherd the early church. He took an old man named Abraham and a harlot named Rahab, a Moabite named Ruth, an adulteress named Bathsheba, and a pregnant virgin named Mary to be in the linage of Christ. Surely, He can use you and me if we will do as they did and learn to operate in faith.

Jeremiah 32:27 (KJV) *27 Behold, I am the LORD, the God of all flesh: is there anything too hard for me?* In case you don't know, the answer is NO! Nothing is too hard, too big, too small, or too important to ever be beyond His ability and compassion. So ask, trust and receive what you need.

Matthew 21:21-22 (KJV) *21 Jesus answered and said unto them, Verily I say unto you, If ye have faith, and doubt not, ye shall not only do this which is done to the fig tree, but also if ye shall say unto this mountain, Be thou removed, and be thou cast into the sea; it shall be done. 22 And all things, whatsoever ye shall ask in prayer, believing, ye shall receive.* There is something to be said for taking the Word literally. Jesus said we could ask and receive and He meant it. He told us to operate in faith. "The issue of Faith pervades every aspect of our relationship with God and our service for Him. Faith is the source of our strength, our provision, our courage, our guidance and our victory over the world system, the flesh and the devil. It is the only thing that can sustain us in the trials and persecutions predicted for the last days." (Lindsey p. 21)

I know that I am saved. If a temptation to sin comes to me, I resist it. The temptation is not in itself sin; it is the devil trying to get me to forget I am the righteousness of God in Christ and yield to sin. It does not mean I am not saved; it means I am being tested. I do not have to frantically grasp for salvation. I am still saved; that is my position. It is not based on my feelings at the time, or my behavior, but is based on what I have believed concerning the work of Christ.

If I resist sin when presented with it, why don't I resist other attacks the same way? When the enemy comes to me with symptoms that say I am sick, I can resist those too. The symptom may be the devil trying to steal my health. I don't have to grasp for healing, because I am already healed. My health was purchased with blood. I have health and healing just like I have salvation; it was purchased for me. It is mine when I feel like it is, and equally mine when I do not feel like it. The Word is stronger evidence than what my body says. I am a believer, and part of what I believe is that the whole of my being was redeemed. In the same way, when I have a financial need, I can go to my Father based upon my relationship and get my need met there. Everything I will ever need is received through faith.

Faith does not have to see to believe. There was a good example in the Old Testament. The king of Israel was angry with Elisha, so he tried to capture him. **II Kings 6:14-17 (KJV)** *14 Therefore sent he thither horses, and chariots, and a great host: and they came by night, and compassed the city about. 15 And when the servant of the man of God was risen early, and gone forth, behold, an host compassed the city both with horses and chariots. And his servant said unto him, Alas, my master! how shall we do? 16 And he answered, Fear not: for they that be with us are more than they that be with them.* That servant thought 'Elisha and me that is only two.' He was operating in the natural. Elisha was seeing in the spirit. He had faith that God was protecting him. *17 And Elisha prayed, and said, LORD, I pray thee, open his eyes, that he may see. And the LORD opened the eyes of the young man; and he saw: and, behold, the mountain was full of horses and chariots of fire round about Elisha.* Elisha did not need to see, because he had confidence in God. Sometime when we walk by faith instead of sight, it is against overwhelming odds, but God is always faithful. We can trust Him no matter how outnumbered we feel.

Elisha had entered into a place of rest that came from knowing the God he served. We can also enter into rest. We start with salvation, but we are to continue to find His peace and assurance to meet all of our needs. **Hebrews 4:9-11 (KJV)** *9 There remaineth therefore a rest to the people of God. 10 For he that is entered into his rest, he also hath ceased from his own works, as God did from his. 11 Let us labour therefore to enter into that rest, lest any man fall after the same example of unbelief.* That rest is primarily us believing His promises. Every man, woman and child can enter that place by faith. "God has established the precedent that the biblical promises made to other people at other times are still available and valid to us. We can claim all of these promises as long as the circumstances and conditions are similar." (Lindsey p. 41) Even when the storms of life rage against us, we are safe in Christ Jesus.

You do not have to fight alone, but you are the only one who can control your fears and trust that God is more than enough for your battle. "The only way to serve God is to see the challenges of living and serving Him in the light of His ability to work through you by His Spirit." (Lindsey p. 75) People with great skills and knowledge are often willing to trust in their own abilities. Sometimes those who do not have as much ability are more willing to be dependent upon Him. It is not the most talented, skilled, or educated who accomplish great things for God. Rather, it is those who are the best at trusting Him who excel in life. **John 3:27 (KJV)** *27 John answered and said, A man can receive nothing, except it be given him from heaven.* That is right; all the good that is in any of us, all our talents and victories are just a gift, implanted by God our Father. We can never accomplish anything that matters unless we rely on Him. That takes all the pressure off. We don't have to achieve anything; we don't have to prove anything. We are not in completion with anyone; we are His children, resting in His ability.

He loves us, warts and all. He will make us able to conquer our own battles, and even the faith we use is a gift. **Romans 12:3 (KJV)** *3 For I say, through the grace given unto me, to every man that is among you, not to think of himself more highly than he ought to think; but to think soberly, according as God hath dealt to every man the measure of faith.* We walk by faith, like every one of those people mentioned in Hebrews chapter 11. We realize that our Lord can and will use men and women just like us. **Hebrews 12:1-3 (KJV)** *1 Wherefore seeing we also are compassed about with so great a cloud of witnesses, let us lay aside every weight, and the sin which doth so easily beset us, and let us run with patience the race that is set before us, 2 Looking unto Jesus the author and finisher of our faith; who for the joy that was set before him endured the cross, despising the shame, and is set down at the right hand of the throne of God. 3 For consider him that endured such contradiction of sinners against himself, lest ye be wearied and faint in your minds.* Trusting in the Lord gives us endurance.

Hebrews 10:35-36 (KJV) *35 Cast not away therefore your confidence, which hath great recompence of* *reward. 36 For ye have need of patience, that, after ye have done the will of God, ye might receive the promise.* I believe like that and hold to the promise regardless of circumstances. The fact that I was redeemed is settled in my heart and mind and spirit. I believe and then I pray knowing the answer will manifest.

Knowing that the Word of God is true in the generic sense does not mean I have done anything with it. I have a head full of natural knowledge, some of it useful and some is not. That isn't faith. Really believing means it affects what I say and do. Faith is taking it into my spirit and applying it to my situation. **Isaiah 26:3-4 (KJV)** *3 Thou wilt keep him in perfect peace, whose mind is stayed on thee: because he trusteth in thee. 4 Trust ye in the LORD for ever: for in the LORD JEHOVAH is everlasting strength:* That peace that comes from casting the whole of our worries and problems on Him is the rest and the strength we need daily.

Isaiah 40:28-31 (KJV) *28 Hast thou not known? hast thou not heard, that the everlasting God, the LORD, the Creator of the ends of the earth, fainteth not, neither is weary? there is no searching of his understanding. 29 He giveth power to the faint; and to them that have no might he increaseth strength. 30 Even the youths shall faint and be weary, and the young men shall utterly fall: 31 But they that wait upon the LORD shall renew their strength; they shall mount up with wings as eagles; they shall run, and not be weary; and they shall walk, and not faint.* He gives us strength and ability, so we can constantly trust in His faithfulness.

Real faith will not take no for an answer. It will not give up or let go of the victory Jesus won. Hold on to the promise God gave you. Never say or do anything that contradicts the word concerning your victory. The Word works; faith works. Get them working for you. It is only when we look at Christ's victory and trust in His Word that we are able to set aside fear and worry. We rest in what He has done, but in order to walk and not faint, we exercise our rights and privileges in Him. We walk by faith, day in and day out and we walk in His victory.

I Am Who God Says I Am

II Corinthians 5:7 (KJV) *7 For we walk by faith, not by sight:*

Not by Sight

When John F. Kennedy Jr. crashed off the cost of Martha's Vineyard in July of 1999, it was all over the news. I remember watching as they broadcast the search efforts. There was nothing wrong with his plane. There was, however, a storm and during that storm he lost visibility. Like so many other pilots, he was not instrument rated. When he could not discern his environment, he became confused. He most likely trusted in his physical senses more than his instruments. Many pilots experience vertigo when they can no longer see natural markers or airport landing strips. He probably believed he was flying toward his destination while the whole time he was flying straight to his death. That kind error is common and often deadly, but it is avoidable.

A pilot in a fog bank can call the tower and get turn by turn instructions, but they have to fight their own instincts and physical sensations in order to obey them and most novice pilots cannot force themselves to do that. "The lost pilot and the troubled Christian have something in common. Both could sail along life's pathway smoothly until the storm came. They were not ready for the troubles they encountered." (Hicks p. 9) Both need to become instrument rated. That is, they prepare. They build their knowledge, and spend time training for what to do in a storm. They learn by experience to rely on the source of knowledge, instead of their own senses. For the pilot, that is their gauges and the words from the control tower. For believers, it is Scripture and direct instructions from the Lord. The more we have to depend upon God, the more we do. When we don't know which way to turn, He does.

II Corinthians 5:7 (KJV) *7 For we walk by faith, not by sight:* Any true believer can tell you that there are times when their path seems smooth and their direction is clear and then there are times when they have no hope other than to trust that the Lord can see what they cannot. It is at those times that having a strong relationship with God and a solid foundation in the Word can help them past the darkness and back into the light.

II Corinthians 4:8-9 (KJV) *8 We are troubled on every side, yet not distressed; we are perplexed, but not in despair; 9 Persecuted, but not forsaken; cast down, but not destroyed;* Paul learned not to let worry and fear stop him. "Worry is a special form of fear. The traditional distinction is that fear is caused by an external source while worry or anxiety is produced from the inside. Yet they produce the same physical responses. Worry is fear that has unpacked its bags and signed a long-term lease. Worry never moves out of its own accord—it has to be evicted. (Ortberg p. 123) It may be true that there is danger all around you, but it doesn't have to get inside you. You operate by faith. **Psalm 91:15 (KJV)** *15 He shall call upon me, and I will answer him: I will be with him in trouble; I will deliver him, and honour him.*

"The toughest battles you will ever fight will be those with your own mind... people cannot out think the devil." (Hicks p. 22) Worry will never help. If we are to win in hard times, we have to get back in the faith realm, where we can defeat the devil every time. We get him to come where we are solidly standing on the Word of God and listening to the Spirit and we will out maneuver him.

Moses once got so depressed and frustrated that he basically told God, "Just kill me now." **Numbers 11:10-15 (KJV)** *10 Then Moses heard the people weep throughout their families, every man in the door of his tent: and the anger of the LORD was kindled greatly; Moses also was displeased. 11 And Moses said unto the LORD, Wherefore hast thou afflicted thy servant? and wherefore have I not found favour in thy sight, that thou layest the burden of all this people upon me? 12 Have I conceived all this people? have I begotten them, that thou shouldest say unto me, Carry them in thy bosom, as a nursing father beareth the sucking child, unto the land which thou swarest unto their fathers? 13 Whence should I have flesh to give unto all this people? for they weep unto me, saying, Give us flesh, that we may eat. 14 I am not able to bear all this people alone, because it is too heavy for me. 15 And if thou deal thus with me, kill me, I pray thee, out of hand, if I have found favour in thy sight; and let me not see my wretchedness.* All those millions of people were depending on him and complaining to him. He must have really been frustrated to say what he did, but any leader can understand why he would feel that way.

"Depression that originates from worry and the stress of life or from a personal attack of Satan or as a result of just everyday living in the devil's world… is a subtle attack upon your soul. Be alert to the first sign of worry or a feeling of heaviness. Recognize the pity party for what it is… Be ready, by being prepared. Know who you are in Christ; Worship and praise continually. You can live free from discouragement and depression." (Hicks p. 27) We can't let fear, depression or worry take us captive. **Romans 6:16 (KJV)** *16 Know ye not, that to whom ye yield yourselves servants to obey, his servants ye are to whom ye obey; whether of sin unto death, or of obedience unto righteousness?* We only have one Lord and His name is Jesus, we do not serve fear and worry and we will not let them have dominion over us. **Romans 8:14 (KJV)** *14 For as many as are led by the Spirit of God, they are the sons of God.*

Faith is standing upon the known will and Word of God and acting as if it is true, even when it does not agree with what is seen with the natural senses. Presumption is just deciding to do what you think is best or just what you want. There is no scriptural support but you act anyway. "Being presumptuous in seeking God's will is the result of overestimating your talents. This is also the sin of pride." (Hicks p. 33) I knew three college students who did that. They decided that they could ask for a huge house near their college. They did not have the money for a down payment, let alone a mortgage. They did not have enough money to even pay the utilities for that house. The house was not even for sale. But because they thought they could get anything they prayed for, the three of them opted out of campus housing for the next semester. They thought they were acting in faith, but the whole time they were in presumption. When the semester started one dropped out of school altogether, one moved in with me, and one moved home with mom. They had tried to force faith where there was no word from the Lord and basis in scripture. You can never manipulate God. That wasn't faith, it was acting foolishly. "If you don't know God's will, be patient; remember faith never struggles, it rests." (Hicks p. 35)

Jesus taught his followers to trust in God. Real confidence in your relationship with God will force out fear and worry. **Matthew 6:25-34 (KJV)** *25 Therefore I say unto you, Take no thought for your life, what ye shall eat, or what ye shall drink; nor yet for your body, what ye shall put on. Is not the life more than meat, and the body than raiment? 26 Behold the fowls of the air: for they sow not, neither do they reap, nor gather into barns; yet your heavenly Father feedeth them. Are ye not much better than they? 27 Which of you by taking thought can add one cubit unto his stature? 28 And why take ye thought for raiment? Consider the lilies of the field, how they grow; they toil not, neither do they spin:29 And yet I say unto you, That even Solomon in all his glory was not arrayed like one of these. 30 Wherefore, if God so clothe the grass of the field, which today is, and tomorrow is cast into the oven, shall he not much more clothe you, O ye of little faith? 31 Therefore take no thought, saying, What shall we eat? or, What shall we drink? or, Wherewithal shall we be clothed? 32 (For after all these things do the Gentiles seek:) for your heavenly Father knoweth that ye have need of all these things.* **33 But seek ye first the kingdom of God, and his righteousness; and all these things shall be added unto you.** *34 Take therefore no thought for the morrow: for the morrow shall take thought for the things of itself. Sufficient unto the day is the evil thereof.*

A missionary was in Nicaragua when he learned that worry was a waste of time. He was going to bed in an adobe home within the missionary compound. The doors were locked and the windows closed. He should have been able to lie down and sleep, but just before he closed his eyes he saw a large South American spider. He could not reach it, but he spent the night fearing it might find its way to him. In the morning, his host came in took a long stick and crushed it. When he did it disintegrated into hundreds of dry dusty particles. The spider was dead, dried and only the form of it remained. His lack of knowledge cost him a night of sleep.

His host recognized the difference between a real threat and a dead one. If we want to do well in life it would benefit us to know our enemy and what he can and can't do. We are to stand strong in faith regardless of the circumstance. When we are well versed in the truth, a lie won't make us fearful.

I once preached a sermon called, Dead Snakes Don't Scare Me. The essence of it was that our Lord has already defeated that old serpent the devil and we don't have to be afraid. Where I go, He goes. I am never alone, never afraid because I know the most powerful One who has ever existed is with me and He loves me. The Bible is full of places where it says "fear not" so let's just obey that. "I think God says fear not so often because fear is the number one reason human beings are tempted to avoid doing what God asks them to do." (Ortberg p.118) **John 16:33 (KJV)** *33 These things I have spoken unto you, that in me ye might have peace. In the world ye shall have tribulation: but be of good cheer; I have overcome the world.*

Twice the disciples went through great storms. Once, Jesus calmed the sea. But in the other instance He let Peter walk on that sea while the wind blew, the waves raged and the thunder roared and all around him.

Mark 4:35-40 (KJV) *35 And the same day, when the even was come, he saith unto them, Let us pass over unto the other side. 36 And when they had sent away the multitude, they took him even as he was in the ship. And there were also with him other little ships. 37 And there arose a great storm of wind, and the waves beat into the ship, so that it was now full. 38 And he was in the hinder part of the ship, asleep on a pillow: and they awake him, and say unto him, Master, carest thou not that we perish? 39 And he arose, and rebuked the wind, and said unto the sea, Peace, be still. And the wind* *ceased, and there was a great calm. 40 And he said unto them, Why are ye so fearful? how is it that ye have no faith?* Sometimes the Lord will calm our storms if we call on Him. Sometimes He will just calm His child and let us see that He can keep us through the darkest night and the roughest seas. Occasionally, He will let us experience the joy of walking upon the troubled seas. Our victory adds to our experience and prepares us for the next storm to come. This time, Peter got to step out of his comfort zone and do what no one had ever done before.

Matthew 14:22-26 (KJV) *22 And straightway Jesus constrained his disciples to get into a ship, and to go before him unto the other side, while he sent the multitudes away. 23 And when he had sent the multitudes away, he went up into a mountain apart to pray: and when the evening was come, he was there alone. 24 But the ship was now in the midst of the sea, tossed with waves: for the wind was contrary. 25 And in the fourth watch of the night Jesus went unto them, walking on the sea. 26 And when the disciples saw him walking on the sea, they were troubled, saying, It is a spirit; and they cried out for fear.* It is three in the morning; they are in a terrible storm, the kind of storm that sailors and fishermen feared. They have no experiential reference for what they see. Jesus is meeting them in the place of their need but He comes unexpectedly, walking upon the water. "Sometimes it takes the eyes of faith to recognize when Jesus is around. Often in the middle of the storm, tormented by waves of disappointment and doubt, we are no better at recognizing His presence than they were." (Ortberg p. 14) **Matthew 14:27-33 (KJV)** *27 But straightway Jesus spake unto them, saying, Be of good cheer; it is I; be not afraid. 28 And Peter answered him and said, Lord, if it be thou, bid me come unto thee on the water.* Peter never said, "That is so cool, I want to try it." What he was saying is, "In the worst of the storm I want to be where you are Jesus, call me to you." That was good advice. When all seems lost and there is no help in the natural find Jesus and get close to Him. There is safety where He is. *29 And he said, Come. And when Peter was come down out of the ship, he walked on the water, to go to Jesus.* Jesus just invited Peter on the adventure of a lifetime, and Peter stepped over the side of the boat. He left behind what little safety he had. He left behind all of his experience and former knowledge. He left his friends quaking in the rain. He turned away from all of it to get near Jesus. Peter was acting as if the water was solid. That is all faith is, just taking God at His Word and acting as if it is true. Peter was walking on the foundation of the truthfulness of Christ. He was able to defy the forces of nature because he truly believed. *30 But when he saw the wind boisterous, he was afraid; and beginning to sink, he cried, saying, Lord, save me. 31 And immediately Jesus stretched forth his hand, and caught him, and said unto him, O thou of little faith, wherefore didst thou doubt? 32 And when they were come into the ship, the wind ceased. 33 Then they that were in the ship came and worshipped him, saying, Of a truth thou art the Son of God.*

"Your boat is whatever represents safety and security to you apart from God himself. Your boat is whatever you are tempted to put your trust in, especially when life gets a little stormy. Your boat is whatever keeps you so comfortable that you don't want to give it up even if it's keeping you from joining Jesus on the waves." (Ortberg p. 17) That security might be keeping you from a miracle, or a great adventure of your own. There is no guarantee that you will be safe even in the boat if the wind is strong enough and the waves are pounding into the boat. You could go down either way. Just like the pilot you have to find a way to resist your own instincts and trust the Lord to get you safely to shore. "Each time you get out of the boat, you become a little more likely to get out the next time. It is not that the fear goes away, but that you get used to living with fear. You realize it does not have the power to destroy you." (Ortberg p.22) It is helpful to remember that Jesus has kept safe you before. You have a 100% survival rate at this point in life. Nothing that could have destroyed you has been able to take you down.

People tend to focus on the fact that Peter sank. If you think he is a failure remember there were eleven other men who never took a single step on those waves. They were much bigger failures because they missed the opportunity for growth. None of them had that special moment of walking with the Lord. Their failure may have been unnoticed, but it hindered them all the same. Only Peter risked it all, and faced a little public shame for his actions. "The worst failure is not to sink in the waves. The worst failure is to never get out of the boat." (Ortberg p.23) Peter did experience the impossible; he walked on the water with Jesus. When he got his eyes off the Lord, he let fear overtake him. Fear wrapped its hand securely around his ankle and tried to take him to the bottom of the sea. He started to go under, but he had enough sense to cry out to the Lord. Jesus took him by the hand, and the two of them walked back to the boat. Jesus responded the moment Peter asked for help. "Whether Peter sank or water-walked depended on whether he focused on the storm or on Jesus. But now he understood his dependence on faith much more deeply than he would have if he had never left the boat. It was his willingness to risk failure that helped him to grow." (Ortberg p.24) Even if Jesus had calmed the storm before Peter got out of the boat, he still would have been doing the impossible. Peter had to learn to walk by faith not by sight and so do we.

I remember a few years back when Buzz and I were given a trip to Bermuda. I diligently searched the internet for things for us to do. This was a once in a lifetime trip and we wanted to make it count. I presented Buzz with all the local opportunities and we chose an activity for each day. On our third day there we went Parasailing. Now I have been a coward my whole life and have feared trying new and adventurous things. But I decided I would do this. One woman on the dock waiting with us was planning to pay the fee just to watch her son go up. She asked me, "Why are you doing this? Aren't you afraid?" I answered her with boldness, "I am over fifty years old, if I don't do it now I might never get to do it." The imagined risk was nothing compared to the experience. When we were safely back on the ship she asked me what I thought and I told her, "I would go again right now if I could." She was so afraid, but because I did it, she did it, and she loved it. Our other adventurous event was helmet diving. I can't see well enough without my glasses to enjoy snorkeling and I really do not swim well either. Our answer was to put on a heavy old-time divers helmet and walk on the bottom of the ocean. I could wear my glasses under the helmet, and we had oxygen so I was comfortable trying it. This was pretty cool too. There were three groups who took turns going down with the guide. While we waited we were allowed to swim or watch on the monitor as others took their turn. Buzz, who swims like a fish, jumped off the boat into that deep ocean water below. I wanted to, but I was so nervous I nearly hyperventilated; I felt like I was drowning in the fear. It was a moment of decision; I could stand on that deck trembling or dive into the ocean. I was pretty sure Buzz loved me enough to save me if I needed it. So I told him, "I really want to jump, but I can't do it alone. Hold my hand and jump and I will have to go." He did and I was fine. Maybe I didn't walk on the water, but I walked on the bottom of the ocean, and I dove off of that deck twelve feet above the water, and I swam in the ocean. For me that was just as terrifying and very rewarding. I trusted in my husband to save me if necessary, but I made it back to the ship on my own. I have had to trust God like I trusted in Buzz. I have had to ignore my fear and step out and do what He asked me to do, and every time it has been worth doing.

We learn to trust God one day at a time, one crisis at a time. We learn by experience and we support our faith with the Word of God. We train on a simulator so we don't crash and burn when the real storms of life come. God works with us daily until we are instrument rated, able to trust when we cannot see, and obey when we have no other assurance but His Spirit whispering directions into our ear. We walk by faith, day in and day out until it becomes so natural that we can do it under any circumstance.

Matthew 8:16 (KJV) *16 When the even was come, they brought unto him many that were possessed with devils: and he cast out the spirits with his word, and healed all that were sick:*

Fear No Devil

As believers, we have the authority to release the prisoners and set the captives free. Part of that power is the right to cast out demons. I am not one of those people who see a devil behind every rock or inspiring every action in this world, but there are still people who have been under the attack of demons and God does not want them left that way.

Webster defines demons as any powerful evil spirit that affects behavior; one who is highly energetic and of a negative influence. Bible dictionaries have a more specific definition. A demon is an inferior deity of bad or evil intent, often translated as devils or unclean spirits. Their definition includes the idea of knowing which means they were often used in fortune telling or by mediums. In Bible times, they were considered to be the spiritual agents acting in all the idol worship and did the bidding of Satan. They spread errors among men trying to seduce believers. Some people are fearful of the devil. Others are ignorant, as if there are not forces of evil to even consider. Both extremes neglect the truth of scripture.

Every demon trembles before the one true God and

His Son, Jesus. According to my sources they had the power to afflict the body, causing diseases and unclean passions. To be possessed by a demon means that the person was under complete control of the demon. His words, actions and intents were all controlled by the evil spirit. There are some clear examples in the Bible of how Jesus dealt with those hard cases.

Mark 5:1-20 (KJV) *1 And they came over unto the other side of the sea, into the country of the Gadarenes.* The Gadarenes was an area near the Sea of Galilee. The nearest big city is over six miles away. So, it was a barren place with small villages nearby. *2 And when he was come out of the ship, immediately there met him out of the tombs a man with an unclean spirit,* A cemetery was a perfect setting for an evil spirit to live. This man was so filled with demons that he lived outside of society in the most unbearable of places. *3 Who had his dwelling among the tombs; and no man could bind him, no, not with chains:* Tombs were often located in the protection of caves and this would have been some shelter from the elements. It is also a picture of how depraved and brutal sin and its minions can become. Here we see a man who is living almost like an animal in the place of the dead, which is exactly the level the devil wants mankind in. Sin brings man to the point of self-destruction and even suicide. *4 Because that he had been often bound with fetters and chains, and the chains had been plucked asunder by him, and the fetters broken in pieces: neither could any man tame him.* He had super human strength. It appears that the locals had tried to restrain him without success. *5 And always, night and day, he was in the mountains, and in the tombs, crying, and cutting himself with stones.* Evil spirits are by nature destructive and this spirit was harming its host. This appears to be a tormenting spirit, which affects the mind and eventually the body as well.

Mark 5:6-20 (KJV) *6 But when he saw Jesus afar off, he ran and worshipped him,* The demon was forced to bow before the One he recognized as God. *7 And cried with a loud voice, and said, What have I to do with thee, Jesus, thou Son of the most high God?* There is no unity between good and evil and the spirit recognized that. *I adjure thee by God, that thou torment me not. 8 For he said unto him, Come out of the man, thou unclean spirit.* Upon contact, the demon is under pressure and the behavior of such a possessed man would get worse. Jesus has already spoken to the demon, not to the man, and commanded that it leave. Jesus has the authority to force them to leave; He has served them an eviction notice. Evidently this possession was so powerful that the results were not immediate. *9 And he asked him, What is thy name? And he answered, saying, My name is Legion: for we are many.* The demons speaking to Christ go back and forth from saying "I to we." They had total control. If the demon speaking was representing what was a Roman legion of soldiers, that would mean 4000-6000 men or in this case evil spirits. That is a powerful force to deal with, but they recognized the authority of Jesus and begged Him not to destroy them. *10 And he besought him much that he would not send them away out of the country.* Demon spirits need a body in order to manifest so they wanted to stay where they were. Their host had been a useful vessel for their evil attacks. There will be a day when every evil spirit and the devil that controls them will be bound and cast into the pit. It will only take one angel to do the job. That day is greatly feared by demons and they may have been speaking of that when they said, don't send us away. *11 Now there was there nigh unto the mountains a great herd of swine feeding. 12 And all the devils besought him, saying, Send us into the swine, that we may enter into them.* Pigs were considered unclean animals, so there was nothing to protect here. Jews should not have been tending that herd or selling them or even touching them. *13 And forthwith Jesus gave them leave. And the unclean spirits went out, and entered into the swine: and the herd ran violently down a steep place into the sea, (they were about two thousand;) and were choked in the sea.* It seems the pigs would rather die than carry the evil spirits around. Death is a natural result of having left all that is holy. Jesus is the way, the truth, and the life. *14 And they that fed the swine fled, and told it in the city, and in the country. And they went out to see what it was that was done. 15 And they come to Jesus, and see him that was possessed with the devil, and had the legion, sitting, and clothed, and in his right mind: and they were afraid.* This is the same man but he is so different now, calm, clothed, and able to speak intelligently again. They are overwhelmed at the differences. *16 And they that saw it told them how it befell to him that was possessed with the devil, and also concerning the swine. 17 And they began to pray him to depart out of their coasts.* You would think they would beg Jesus to stay but they wanted this Man with such power to go away. *18 And when he was come into the ship, he that had been possessed with the devil prayed him that he might be with him. 19 Howbeit Jesus suffered him not, but saith unto him, Go home to thy friends, and tell them how great things the Lord hath done for thee, and hath had compassion on thee. 20 And he departed, and began to publish in Decapolis how great things Jesus had done for him: and all men did marvel.* The man was set free and he told everyone he met that Jesus had healed and restored him. The next time Jesus came to visit in this area, the people were ready for Him. This man, once as good as dead, had become a powerful influence that prepared the way for them to receive the Lord Jesus.

The Apostles, including Paul, used the same power

of the Holy Spirit to force demons to leave the oppressed and possessed. They based their faith on the One who had all authority and delegated it to them and they cast out devils. **Acts 16:16-18 (KJV)** *16 And it came to pass, as we went to prayer, a certain damsel possessed with a spirit of divination met us, which brought her masters much gain by soothsaying: 17 The same followed Paul and us, and cried, saying, These men are the servants of the most high God, which shew unto us the way of salvation. 18 And this did she many days.* The words she spoke were true but the influence that caused her to speak was evil. *But Paul, being grieved, turned and said to the spirit, I command thee in the name of Jesus Christ to come out of her. And he came out the same hour.* For his trouble, Paul was beaten and imprisoned.

There is power to defeat the devil in the name of Jesus, but it is delegated to those bought by the blood of Jesus—those born into His family. The believers had a right to use the name of Jesus and the power attached to His victory to force devils to leave. **Acts 19:13-16 (KJV)** *13 Then certain of the vagabond Jews, exorcists, took upon them to call over them which had evil spirits the name of the Lord Jesus, saying, We adjure you by Jesus whom Paul preacheth. 14 And there were seven sons of one Sceva, a Jew, and chief of the priests, which did so. 15 And the evil spirit answered and said, Jesus I know, and Paul I know; but who are ye? 16 And the man in whom the evil spirit was leaped on them, and overcame them, and prevailed against them, so that they fled out of that house naked and wounded.* Believers were given the authority to cast out demons. Every spirit being is aware of the presence of Christ within the believer. They also saw a lack of connection between God and these men who were using the name of Jesus without having a relationship with him. Demons are no match for our Lord, but they are nothing to be trifled with either. We know Jesus cast out demons. The disciples cast out demons, and early believers saw this as part of their ministry.

Mark 16:15 & 17 (KJV) *15 And he said unto them, Go ye into all the world, and preach the gospel to every creature. & 17 And these signs shall follow them that believe; In my name shall they cast out devils;* None of that great commission has lessened over time. We still have the mission to minister to both Christians and unbelievers.

We are fully equipped to represent Jesus as He was and is. We are more than able to bring healing to the sick, salvation to the lost and deliverance to all who are oppressed. Our Lord is the One with the power and He has given it to us. There have been times when I was part of a ministry teem that cast out destructive demons. Actual demon possession is very rare. But all evil can be traced to demonic influence.

I know that you can fight off the devil by taking authority over him because it has worked for me. When I had my first real job, I worked in a bridal shop as a saleswoman and seamstress. One day a very tall man came into the shop and asked to see some wedding dresses for his fiancé, who lived in another state. After selecting one, he made an unusual request that I model the gown. The owner said it was a reasonable request and to comply, which I did. On his next visit, he asked to try on a gown himself, which was both strange and totally unacceptable. He said he had lied before and was in a play and needed a dress and matching shoes. He made everyone very uncomfortable. After his third trip in, we decided he should shop elsewhere and I asked him to leave. The following morning I came in early and opened the shop. I always arrived first and was used to being alone until we opened. When I had unlocked the doors, I began working in the cutting room. I heard the bell on the front door. We were not technically open, but I went out expecting a customer. There stood that same man. "Can I help you?" I asked. He walked up to me, got in my face and with an angry, raspy voice said, "We are going into the fitting room." I responded, "I don't think so." He pulled out a rope, wound it around both fists, placed it at my throat and said in a louder, more persistent voice, "We are going into the back room." None of the images in my mind about his intentions seemed good. In that moment I heard these words come out of my spirit, that place where the Spirit of Truth dwells, "In the name of Jesus Christ whose I am and whom I serve, I command every foul spirit to leave." The Holy Spirit who rose up within me was full of authority. With the power of His presence, I backed that attacker out the door and he ran away. It was not my size that sent him running for the door. He stood a good foot taller than me and outweighed me by at least 50 pounds of sheer muscle. But I stood in the authority that was delegated to me as a member of the body of Christ. I claimed my relationship with Him and the enemy ran. My boss came in shortly after that and when she heard what had happened she called the police. They never did catch him, but I was never afraid, because the One who bought me with His own blood gave me the authority to defeat the enemy when he came to steal, kill, and destroy. **Ephesians 3:11-12 (KJV)** *11 According to the eternal purpose which he purposed in Christ Jesus our Lord: 12 In whom we have boldness and access with confidence by the faith of him.* My boldness did indeed come from Him.

As believers we can come with full assurance against any evil force and trust that the Lord stands with us and lives in us and we can overcome whatever we face in life. No devil is a match for the blood.

Matthew 5:13-14 (KJV) *13 Ye are the salt of the earth: but if the salt have lost his savour, wherewith shall it be salted? it is thenceforth good for nothing, but to be cast out, and to be trodden under foot of men. 14 Ye are the light of the world. A city that is set on an hill cannot be hid.*

Salt & Light

Jesus often used parables and object lessons to teach difficult concepts. Immediately after the beatitudes, we hear the Lord speaking to His disciples that they are salt and light. In a way, this is a continuation of His teaching on the attitude and the influence His true believers should exhibit. The scripture indicates that the Lord sat down to teach, and then His closest followers formed a circle around Him. Just beyond that circle, a multitude gathered to glean wisdom from the Teacher. Here He takes two common elements from everyday life and makes them into solid examples to teach His true followers.

In order to do justice to the two statements, you are salt and you are light, we need the context. I trust that you will indulge me in touching lightly on those first few verses to get us to our destination. **Matthew 5:3-6 (KJV)** *3 Blessed are the poor in spirit: for theirs is the kingdom of heaven.* That word blessed, implies that those people are favored by God. That is to say, happy, and to be envied are those with all of these characteristics. First, He mentions those who recognize they don't have it all figured out and are in need spiritually. Only the one who knows they need salvation will accept a Savior who purchased it for them. Once we know we need God and are willing to see ourselves as loved by God, but still separated from Him, we can come to Him. We are blessed when poor in spirit, because only then we can be born again—then the kingdom of heaven is ours. *4 Blessed are they that mourn: for they shall be comforted.* I think of this one in two distinctly different ways. One, the verse is still concerning the lost seeking salvation. If we mourn over the fact that we are without God and without hope outside of Jesus, we will repent. **II Corinthians 7:10 (KJV)** *10 For godly sorrow worketh repentance to salvation not to be repented of...* We will receive and though our sorrow was evidence of our lost state, the entrance of peace and comfort is evidence of our salvation. "Jesus' blood did the job once and for all, and you are free from sin. Because God declared it so, you are the righteousness of God and you have the right to be cleansed. (Dollar p. 33) I also think that this refers to any kind of loss and the grief that follows. When we mourn, Jesus will bring us comfort. He will restore our hope, our peace and our joy. The Lord shows His beloved the way out of the valley. *5 Blessed are the meek: for they shall inherit the earth.* Meekness and humility are words that have lost their meanings in our society. To be meek or humble does not mean to put yourself down, or to think poorly of yourself. It means to have an honest estimate of your own ability and to see your strengths and your limitations and to be both teachable and submissive to the One who can make you more. God wants us to have a changeable attitude, a potential for growth. It is the world's way to assert yourself and push your way forward, but it is God's way to accept His will and in doing so to possess all and eventually to rule and reign with Him. *6 Blessed are they which do hunger and thirst after righteousness: for they shall be filled.* Those who want the character of God, His righteousness, will be satisfied. To hunger and thirst after God and His ways, means

He is your motivation. His presence and His will are your passion. When we want God like we want water on a hot day, we will be satisfied. That reminds me of David in **Psalm 42:1-2 (KJV)** *1 As the hart panteth after the water brooks, so panteth my soul after thee, O God. 2 My soul thirsteth for God, for the living God: when shall I come and appear before God?* That kind of passion will never be denied.

Blessed, happy and to be envied are those who show kindness and mercy to others. **Matthew 5:7-8 (KJV)** *7 Blessed are the merciful: for they shall obtain mercy.* That is the idea behind the golden rule and reaping what you sow. But know this, mercy came to you when you were deserving of judgment and punishment. You give mercy because you did not deserve mercy or forgiveness yet God gave it to you. All the recipients of mercy owe it to the undeserving around them. A constant outflow of mercy in your life means you have room for more to flow into your life. *8 Blessed are the pure in heart: for they shall see God.* Purity of heart is almost beyond our comprehension. A heart that is like God, with nothing in it that opposes Him or thinks evil of others, is truly a rare treasure. This verse really sums up all those before it. A pure heart is a heart that is full of love. It means we are like God who is perfect love. A pure heart is unclouded by greed or lust or fear or jealousy. A heart that is born from above is our only hope for a pure heart.

The next attitude we are to exhibit is that of a peacemaker. Paul has a whole list of attitude adjustments for believers in his letter to the Romans. I recommend reading the whole chapter, but I want to add just one verse here. **Romans 12:18 (KJV)** *18 If it be possible, as much as lieth in you, live peaceably with all men.* Sometimes we can bring peace to a volatile situation because the Lord has given us a peace that passes all understanding. Let's get back to those beatitudes. **Matthew 5:9 (KJV)** *9 Blessed are the peacemakers: for they shall be called the children of God.* Bringing peace is evidence of God within us. It is allowing His love and grace to be magnified in the earth. He gave us peace when we were enemies to God. He found a way to bridge the gap between our sinful lives and His holiness. He reached out for us and loved us beyond any reasonable expectation and made us one with Him. We are here to show that kind of grace and mercy and compassion to the broken of this world. The world we live in is full of chaos and violence and hatred. Those we encounter are desperate for a moment of peace and an ambassador of hope. Any time we bring peace in the face of turmoil, we look like our Father.

Matthew 5:10-12 (KJV) *10 Blessed are they which are persecuted for righteousness' sake: for theirs is the kingdom of heaven.* Jesus was the first to experience the fullness of persecution because He was righteous. He faced the cross not because He was a sinner but because He wanted to set sinners free. He died because we needed a Savior. He suffered in our place and in doing so made us acceptable to God. He died to make us righteous. *11 Blessed are ye, when men shall revile you, and persecute you, and shall say all manner of evil against you falsely, for my sake. 12 Rejoice, and be exceeding glad: for great is your reward in heaven: for so persecuted they the prophets which were before you.* We are united to Jesus in His suffering and in our own from time to time. We are to express His nature and His character no matter what comes in our lives. We are called to live above offense and allow others the same grace we received, even if we suffer because of it.

As Christians, we have an influence in this fallen

world. We are both salt and light. We desire to represent Him in such a way that the world will want Him. We make the world tolerable and show the lost the way to Jesus. That is a tall order.

Matthew 5:13 (KJV) *13 Ye are the salt of the earth: but if the salt have lost his savour, wherewith shall it be salted? it is thenceforth good for nothing, but to be cast out, and to be trodden under foot of men.* When I first read that I thought about seasoning. Christians give the world flavor. Salt was considered so vitally important that people were actually paid wages in salt. Salt had to be mined from places like the Dead Sea, dried and carried inland. It was then saturated in water and the sand and debris was removed. Salt was vital for cooking but it had a few other uses. It was a preservative. Before there was refrigeration, meat and fish were salted to keep them safe to eat over extended time periods. Salt also cleanses and purifies wounds. We are that cleansing agent. We keep the evil from overtaking this world. Believers make the world tolerable. Our lives are a preserving force to transform and balance the lost and sinful ones around us. We keep corruption from taking over. As salt, we can never let the world influence us to the point of becoming like them. We must make a difference and show a distinction. As long as we represent the Lord, we are showing a better more tasteful and enduring life. Believers give the world hope. We are the salt; we carry the zest of eternal life.

Next, the Lord said we were light. **Matthew 5:14-16 (KJV)** *14 Ye are the light of the world. A city that is set on an hill cannot be hid. 15 Neither do men light a candle, and put it under a bushel, but on a candlestick; and it giveth light unto all that are in the house. 16 Let your light so shine* *before men, that they may see your good works, and glorify your Father which is in heaven. Jesus also said He was light.* **John 8:12 (KJV)** *12 Then spake Jesus again unto them, saying, I am the light of the world: he that followeth me shall not walk in darkness, but shall have the light of life. And in the next chapter He spoke it again.* **John 9:5 (KJV)** *5 As long as I am in the world, I am the light of the world.* Jesus is like the sun; He produces light. He alone is the true light that shines. We however, are like the moon, we do not produce light; we reflect it. He is the light of the world and we show them His glory. Light can never be hidden. No amount of darkness can extinguish even the tiniest flame from a candle. Light dispenses and dispossesses all that is not light.

In Him is light and life. **I John 1:5-7 (KJV)** *5 This then is the message which we have heard of him, and declare unto you, that God is light, and in him is no darkness at all. 6 If we say that we have fellowship with him, and walk in darkness, we lie, and do not the truth: 7 But if we walk in the light, as he is in the light, we have fellowship one with another, and the blood of Jesus Christ his Son cleanseth us from all sin.* It is our obligation to reflect His light, and to walk in what it illuminates before us.

God uses us to reveal Himself to men to enlighten their senses so they will seek Him. We are a shining example of the life that He alone can give. We light the way. We show them there is hope; we keep men from falling into the potholes of life. We become a reflection of Christ and His light so that all who see us can find their way to Him. Never be ashamed of the presence of God in you. Show the world who He is, and live in the brightness He has produced in you. We were once living in darkness and sin, but no longer. We were once afraid, bitter, and worried, but now we have peace. We are on display, to make sure that darkness never wins. We are here to show them there is a better way. Let your light shine brightly.

I Corinthians 15:54-55 (NIV) *54 When the perishable has been clothed with the imperishable, and the mortal with immortality, then the saying that is written will come true: "Death has been swallowed up in victory." 55 "Where, O death, is your victory? Where, O death, is your sting?"*

Resurrection Power

    A few years ago, Buzz and I were driving out west and we decided to stop at the memorial for Custer's Last Stand...The Battle of the Little Bighorn. We heard a grandson of one of the women who was there that day. She was a little girl during the battle. While they were preparing breakfast, Custer and the U.S. Army descended upon the village. The man who was telling the story told us that many in the tribe were killed in the ambush. He shared details about their culture while standing in front of a teepee like the one his grandmother had slept in that morning. She survived because she was out drawing water for the family. She hid during the battle. Custer's army was there to force the Sioux and several other Native American tribes onto reservations; he had orders to kill any who resisted. It was a fierce battle, and a horrible massacre of women and children. Most of the men were not in camp when the soldiers came. The warriors returned to the carnage and retaliated. There were many lives taken that day on both sides. Instead of Custer's predicted victory, the Army lost the battle and Custer and his men were slaughtered. The story was fascinating. There was a museum and teepees and all of it was interesting. But the most impressive thing we saw was the hill where Custer died. It wasn't a formal cemetery. There were no nice neat rows of headstones. Just small markers scattered around. The bodies of soldiers had been buried where they fell. They were strewn here and there. The General and the lowest infantry soldier were buried in the places where they died and there was something about seeing them like that. It was as if there was no honor for them. It appeared as if they were in such a hurry they could not bury them well. But maybe more than that it was a testimony as to where they had stood and fought. It was a killing field and anyone could see the devastation that occurred there.

In the Bible I read about another place where the dead were just left in the place they died. **Ezekiel 37:1-13 (KJV)** *1 The hand of the LORD was upon me, and carried me out in the spirit of the LORD, and set me down in the midst of the valley which was full of bones,* If it is the valley of dry bones it is because all of the fallen have been dead for a long time *2 And caused me to pass by them round about: and, behold, there were very many in the open valley; and, lo, they were very dry.* The prophet was walking around in the middle of that valley. It was a graveyard, more accurately it was probably a battlefield. Some place where they had fought and died and not even been buried. It was like that hill where we stood overlooking the markers of Custer and his men. Long past, long dead, these bones were all that was left of what had been real lives. It was impossible to tell which bones belonged to a single skeleton. There had been animal predators and weather to cause the full decay and scattering of what had been human bodies. They were almost but not quite forgotten. *3 And he said unto me, Son of man, can these bones live? And I answered, O Lord GOD, thou knowest.* The prophet said that only God could know what potential there is in something so dead. But it also said in verse 1 that God's hand was upon Ezekiel. It was not his ability, his past experiences; it was the Lord directing and touching and carrying Ezekiel that brought him to this dead place. Is there any hope for these?

Can life come where death has reigned? It was a question that we may have asked at one time or another about a part of our life, or a part of our anointing. It might be a question about someone we had seen fall to the ground wounded and damaged and who appeared to have let the life of God bleed out of them. Only where death has reigned can there be a resurrection. God wanted the prophet to see beyond the obvious, beyond the natural, into the place where faith connected with the author of life itself.

Ezekiel 37:4-8 (KJV) *4 Again he said unto me, Prophesy upon these bones, and say unto them, O ye dry bones, hear the word of the LORD. 5 Thus saith the Lord GOD unto these bones; Behold, I will cause breath to enter into you, and ye shall live: 6 And I will lay sinews upon you, and will bring up flesh upon you, and cover you with skin, and put breath in you, and ye shall live; and ye shall know that I am the LORD.* He said I brought you here and I commanded you to walk where the dead are, and now I am asking you to speak life to them. It was a tall order. It took stepping out beyond the normal area of faith. It was asking for more than one miracle. The Amplified Bible says, *"I will lay sinews upon you, and will bring up flesh upon you and cover you with skin, and put breath and spirit in you, and you [dry bones] shall live; and you shall know, understand and realize, that I am the Lord [the Sovereign Ruler, calling forth loyalty and obedient service.]"* They were so dead it was just bones, just a remnant of what had been. It took a creative miracle just to begin. Ezekiel had nothing to work with except the Word of the Lord and that was more than enough. *7 So I prophesied as I was commanded: and as I prophesied, there was a noise, and behold a shaking, and the bones came together, bone to his bone. 8 And when I beheld, lo, the sinews and the flesh came up upon them, and the skin covered them above: but there was no breath in them.*

The entire death and decay process was reversed. The bones reconnected, the rotten flesh and decay were gone, the bodies were restored; they looked good but they were still dead. No matter how good you look on the outside it is the spirit of God on the inside that brings life. You can dress up a dead body but it is still dead. I have only heard of one man with enough faith to walk into a funeral home and pull a body out of the casket and command it to live. That man was Smith Wigglesworth, the plumber turned evangelist in the early 1900's. He was documented to have raised five people from the dead, including one who had been embalmed, and laid out in his casket. That is powerful faith. It is God directed faith with God's own authority behind it. That does not happen by the will of man. The thing God was speaking to Ezekiel does not happen without the Lord either.

Ezekiel 37:9-10 (KJV) *9 Then said he unto me, Prophesy unto the wind, prophesy, son of man, and say to the wind, Thus saith the Lord GOD; Come from the four winds, O breath, and breathe upon these slain, that they may live.* The Lord told Ezekiel to prophesy. He said speak to that dead bunch and command the wind to blow. He was told to speak for the breath of God to be restored in them. *10 So I prophesied as he commanded me, and the breath came into them, and they lived, and stood up upon their feet, an exceeding great army.* I can imagine that killing field once soaked with their blood giving up its captives. I can see them standing there ready to fight again. Only God can do that.

Ezekiel 37:11-14 (KJV) *11 Then he said unto me, Son of man, these bones are the whole house of Israel: behold, they say, Our bones are dried, and our hope is lost: we are cut off for our parts.* The whole of the church has been weary and broken and under siege. The bodies of believers were sick and damaged and the doctors gave their report that hope was gone, but God still has a say. *12 Therefore prophesy and say unto them, Thus saith the Lord GOD; Behold, O my people, I will open your graves, and cause you to come up out of your graves, and bring you into the land of Israel. 13 And ye shall know that I am the LORD, when I have opened your graves, O my people, and brought you up out of your graves, 14 And shall put my spirit in you, and ye shall live, and I shall place you in your own land: then shall ye know that I the LORD have spoken it, and performed it, saith the LORD.* Come up out of the pit and out of that valley. Come up out of the graveyard. Let the dead things go, leave them behind.

Sometimes it gets worse before it gets better. Just what did we expect to find by lying down and giving up? There is no quit in us. There is no place where we can just let the world go by as if we don't care and nothing matters. People matter; stuff matters. Your relationship with God deeply matters. Look out the window and see all the people, almost everyone you see is the walking dead. If they aren't born again, they are still dead in sin and dead men have no future. Walk into any hospital or funeral parlor and see the power of death at work. It is so sad that sin and death have the ability to destroy the ones we love. As a whole the body of Christ, the church, has been acting like the walking dead. You are not some zombie.

Have you ever read about the anointing that lingered in the bones of the prophet Elisha? **II Kings 13:20-21 (KJV)** *20 And Elisha died, and they buried him. And the bands of the Moabites invaded the land at the coming in of the year. 21 And it came to pass, as they were burying a man, that, behold, they spied a band of men; and they cast the man into the sepulchre of Elisha: and when the man was let down, and touched the bones of Elisha, he revived, and stood up on his feet.* There was so much of God in the man that even his dead dry bones possessed a powerful anointing. If a dead prophet under the Old Covenant had that kind of power residing in his bones, just imagine the power in the living believer.

Get up out of that dead place. Throw off the smelly rags that stink of death; you are alive. You get up and nothing dead comes with you. The same Lord who saved you is still speaking life to the dead. Jesus healed you, breathed into you so He can call out of you what He is and that resurrection life in you is full of power. He that is life, poured out his life on the cross, so you could live victorious. You have resureection life in you.

Psalm 23:1-6 (KJV) *1 The LORD is my shepherd; I shall not want. 2 He maketh me to lie down in green pastures: he leadeth me beside the still waters. 3 He restoreth my soul: he leadeth me in the paths of righteousness for his name's sake.* God is providing for me, I rest refreshed and I have all I need to eat and drink and He renews and restores my weary mind and the depths of my soul and spirit. He guides me day in and day out, and He orders my steps. I can walk as the righteous, because He has made me to be righteous. *4 Yea, though I walk through the valley of the shadow of death, I will fear no evil: for thou art with me; thy rod and thy staff they comfort me.* Sometimes you have to go through the valley of the shadow of death so you can walk out on the other side. It is for the Father's glory. And it is only a shadow of death; real death has already been defeated. *5 Thou preparest a table before me in the presence of mine enemies:* Right there where the enemy thought I had lost all, right there where my broken and damaged body lay looking all dead and decayed, the Lord honored me, blessed me, fed me and made me his own. *thou anointest my head with oil; my cup runneth over.* To make the cup to run over was to invite the one it was poured out for, to stay forever. *6 Surely goodness and mercy shall follow me all the days of my life: and I will dwell in the house of the LORD forever.* Eternal life is the true victory over physical death.

I Corinthians 15:54-55 (NIV) *54 When the perishable has been clothed with the imperishable, and the mortal with immortality, then the saying that is written will come true: "Death has been swallowed up in victory." 55 "Where, O death, is your victory? Where, O death, is your sting?"* The Message Bible says, "Death who is afraid of you now?" It was the One with resurrection life that spoke to death as if it was nothing.

Speaking to what is dead and dry to come alive has no potential of victory unless it is God who speaks. If God is speaking, nothing dead stays dead. If it is God speaking, then there isn't anything or anyone who can resist His words. He can make you live where there was no chance, no hope.

If it is Lazarus who lay in the grave or the widow's son on his way to be buried or Jairus' daughter being resurrected, it is because recently there was a death and a loss. Loss and death will try to take us to the place of no return but death is not the final word for the believer. **John 11:25-26 (KJV)**

25 Jesus said unto her, I am the resurrection, and the life: he that believeth in me, though he were dead, yet shall he live: 26 And whosoever liveth and believeth in me shall never die. Believest thou this? She said yes, she believed, I believe too.

Do you know why the Romans were so afraid of Jesus? He could heal anyone sick or wounded. He could feed an entire army with a few pieces of bread and fish. He could give life back to the one who was dead. There was no way to defeat Him. They nailed Jesus to a cross and thought they had put an end to him. They lay him in a grave and said, "We will never see Him again." But He rose, victorious. He who is resurrection life can and will change what has been dead. His life is in you. Your life is hidden in Him. He has given all power to the believer. The devil should quake in fear when you rise up and pray in faith.

I Corinthians 2:7-10 (KJV) *7 But we speak the wisdom of God in a mystery, even the hidden wisdom, which God ordained before the world unto our glory: 8 Which none of the princes of this world knew: for had they known it, they would not have crucified the Lord of glory.* The devil didn't know that bringing Jesus to death would defeat death. He didn't know that resurrection life would not just restore the Messiah, but would restore every man to ever believe in Him. *9 But as it is written, Eye hath not seen, nor ear heard, neither have entered into the heart of man, the things which God hath prepared for them that love him. 10 But God hath revealed them unto us by his Spirit: for the Spirit searcheth all things, yea, the deep things of God.* The power of the cross is not just that sin is gone and judgment will not fall upon you. It is that you can walk free in life. The power of the cross is that REAL LIFE is yours—that His resurrection life is in you now. You have life inside.

There is coming a day when the slain of the battlefield and those buried in the grave will hear the Lord call. It will be greater than what happened in Ezekiel's day. In that day, bone and flesh that have been long dead will come together and form new resurrected bodies.

I Thessalonians 4:13-17 (KJV) *13 But I would not have you to be ignorant, brethren, concerning them which are asleep, that ye sorrow not, even as others which have no hope. 14 For if we believe that Jesus died and rose again, even so them also which sleep in Jesus will God bring with him. 15 For this we say unto you by the word of the Lord, that we which are alive and remain unto the coming of the Lord shall not prevent them which are asleep. 16 For the Lord himself shall descend from heaven with a shout, with the voice of the archangel, and with the trump of God: and the dead in Christ shall rise first: 17 Then we which are alive and remain shall be caught up together with them in the clouds, to meet the Lord in the air: and so shall we ever be with the Lord.* Every vaporized body from the World Trade Centers will come together. Every bit of bone and flesh that ever lived will hear the voice of the Lord calling life into them. Every sailor buried at sea will come up out of that ocean; my dad will rise up out of the cemetery. No part of death will be able to hold them back. They are already marked for resurrection.

You are marked for resurrection. You are the born-again. As the resurrected while still living, there is nothing damaged that can't be made whole. Where there was lack there can be provision. We are not finished. If your life was a book or a movie no one has said THE END. While we are on this earth we are here to be a resurrected army ready to fight again, able to withstand any assault. We are empowered by the Spirit of the Living God. There is resurrection life in us.

Psalm 107:2 (KJV) *2 Let the redeemed of the LORD say so, whom he hath redeemed from the hand of the enemy;*

Who do you say you are?

Now, just who do you say that you are? Are you the saying what God has already spoken over you? He says you are His beloved, His bride, His child. God calls you redeemed. He said you were chosen, wanted and made righteous. "If you believe you are the righteousness of God, it will move you to begin exercising your rights." (Dollar p. 11)

As His children, born again by faith in His incredible sacrifice, we are to declare our relationship. We are to rejoice in our oneness. We are to tell everyone we belong to the Most High. **Psalm 107:2 (KJV)** *2 Let the redeemed of the LORD say so, whom he hath redeemed from the hand of the enemy;* We are the redeemed.

Revelation 12:11 (KJV) *11 And they overcame him by the blood of the Lamb, and by the word of their testimony; and they loved not their lives unto the death.* Our reference to ourselves should always be one of victory, because we are blood bought. We are brought into the kingdom by our conquering King, Jesus. We can shout it; declare it before men and angels and demons. We are His.

I Corinthians 1:30 (KJV) *30 But of him are ye in Christ Jesus, who of God is made unto us wisdom, and righteousness, and sanctification, and redemption:* We were legally set free, declared not guilty, pardoned. All of our sins and debts are paid in full. When Jesus suffered and died it was not for Himself, but for us. We were there at the cross, carried in the heart of our Lord. We were dying with Him. We were resurrected with Christ. We are free because He purchased our release. "I realized that no matter what I had done, the blood of Jesus is strong enough to deal with my sin, and strong enough to maintain the righteousness of God in my life. Now nothing is impossible to me and I can conquer anything that life throws at me. The same is true for you." (Dollar p.66)

Hebrews 10:14-17 (KJV) *14 For by one offering he hath perfected for ever them that are sanctified. 15 Whereof the Holy Ghost also is a witness to us: for after that he had said before, 16 This is the covenant that I will make with them after those days, saith the Lord, I will put my laws into their hearts, and in their minds will I write them; 17 And their sins and iniquities will I remember no more.* "The words 'no more' are a strong double negative in the original Greek text. In other words, God is saying, 'Your sins I will by no means ever remember!' He remembered yours sins 2000 years ago at the cross." (Prince 1/3/18) Every sin past, present and future was forever paid for and we go free. Jesus died that we would never be sin conscious again. At every moment we can look at the cross and see we are already free. The blood that saved us, keeps us. That blood was more than enough. He did not save us to leave us damaged and weak and lowly. Jesus has lifted us to a higher position.

We are royalty, priestly, powerful; we are His church. **I Peter 2:9 (KJV)** *9 But ye are a chosen generation, a royal priesthood, an holy nation, a peculiar people; that ye should shew forth the praises of him who hath called you out of darkness into his marvellous light:*

God loves us deeply. **Ephesians 1:3-6 (MSG)** *3 How blessed is God! And what a blessing he is! He's the Father of our Master, Jesus Christ, and takes us to the high places of blessing in him. 4 Long before he laid down earth's foundations, he had us in mind, had settled on us as the focus of his love, to be made whole and holy by his love. 5 Long, long ago he decided to adopt us into his family through Jesus Christ. (What pleasure he took in planning this!) 6 He wanted us to enter into the celebration of his lavish gift-giving by the hand of his beloved Son.* There is something wonderful and peaceful and solid in knowing how very much we are loved.

God called us His children; we belong in the family. **Romans 8:14-17 (KJV)** *14 For as many as are led by the Spirit of God, they are the sons of God. 15 For ye have not received the spirit of bondage again to fear; but ye have received the Spirit of adoption, whereby we cry, Abba, Father. 16 The Spirit itself beareth witness with our spirit, that we are the children of God: 17 And if children, then heirs; heirs of God, and joint-heirs with Christ.* Abba is a familiar term; we call Him Daddy. He does not expect us to act like distant relatives. He wants us to come boldly to Him and climb up in His lap and throw our arms around Him and pour out our love on Him.

God calls you saved, healed, delivered and free by virtue of relationship with the Son of God who rescued you from all bondage. **Romans 5:11 (NLT)** *11 So now we can* *rejoice in our wonderful new relationship with God because our Lord Jesus Christ has made us friends of God.* We are welcome where He is. He has entered into a binding covenant with us. We are not casual acquaintances; we are His covenant partners and closest friends.

Song of Songs 6:3 (KJV) *3 I am my beloved's, and my beloved is mine...* Look what it says about us belonging to God in the Old Testament. **Deuteronomy 32: 9 (KJV)** *9 For the LORD'S portion is his people;* We are His portion, His inheritance. God calls us His own people, precious and desirable and we are exactly who He says we are. He calls us His beloved and His friends.

Malachi 3:16-17 (KJV) *16 Then they that feared the LORD spake often one to another: and the LORD hearkened, and heard it, and a book of remembrance was written before him for them that feared the LORD, and that thought upon his name. 17 And they shall be mine, saith the LORD of hosts, in that day when I make up my jewels; and I will spare them, as a man spareth his own son that serveth him.* Our names are in His book.

He calls us light. Believers bring hope to the people of the world and lead them out of darkness. **Matthew 5:14-16 (KJV)** *14 Ye are the light of the world. A city that is set on an hill cannot be hid. 15 Neither do men light a candle, and put it under a bushel, but on a candlestick; and it giveth light unto all that are in the house. 16 Let your light so shine before men, that they may see your good works, and glorify your Father which is in heaven.*

Our self-image is no small thing. When Moses sent out spies into the Promised Land, they came back with what

God called an evil report. Why was it evil? It was evil in that it disagreed with what God had already said. They said, "We can't defeat our enemies they are too strong for us." **Numbers 13:33 (KJV)** *33 And there we saw the giants, the sons of Anak, which come of the giants: and we were in our own sight as grasshoppers, and so we were in their sight.* They were already defeated in their hearts and minds and it made them cowards. Only two men out of that original twelve were allowed to live long enough to see the victory and live in the land. This was their report. **Numbers 14:6-9 (KJV)** *6 And Joshua the son of Nun, and Caleb the son of Jephunneh, which were of them that searched the land, rent their clothes: 7 And they spake unto all the company of the children of Israel, saying, The land, which we passed through to search it, is an exceeding good land. 8 If the LORD delight in us, then he will bring us into this land, and give it us; a land which floweth with milk and honey. 9 Only rebel not ye against the LORD, neither fear ye the people of the land; for they are bread for us: their defence is departed from them, and the LORD is with us: fear them not.* They lived in the blessing and the victory because they said what God had said. Joshua and Caleb believed God and declared His words. So whose report will you echo? Are you who the world says you are? You are wise if you agree you are who God has already said you are.

I John 4:10 (KJV) *10 Herein is love, not that we loved God, but that he loved us, and sent his Son to be the propitiation for our sins.* He so dearly loved us, and His love motivated Him to save us and enter into a relationship with us. The Lord is forever drawing us unto Himself. He did not wait for us to invite Him into our lives, but actively sought us out and purchased us with the blood of Jesus. **Romans 5:8 (KJV)** *8 But God commendeth his love toward us, in* *that, while we were yet sinners, Christ died for us.* Our love for Jesus is a response for such unmerited favor and such sacrificial love. **I John 4:19 (KJV)** *19 We love him, because he first loved us.*

Jesus prayed for his disciples. He did not pray for the twelve alone but also for us. **John 17:11-26 (KJV)** *11 And now I am no more in the world, but these are in the world, and I come to thee. Holy Father, keep through thine own name those whom thou hast given me, that they may be one, as we are. 12 While I was with them in the world, I kept them in thy name: those that thou gavest me I have kept, and none of them is lost, but the son of perdition; that the scripture might be fulfilled. 13 And now come I to thee; and these things I speak in the world, that they might have my joy fulfilled in themselves. 14 I have given them thy word; and the world hath hated them, because they are not of the world, even as I am not of the world. 15 I pray not that thou shouldest take them out of the world, but that thou shouldest keep them from the evil. 16 They are not of the world, even as I am not of the world. 17 Sanctify them through thy truth: thy word is truth. 18 As thou hast sent me into the world, even so have I also sent them into the world. 19 And for their sakes I sanctify myself, that they also might be sanctified through the truth. 20 Neither pray I for these alone, but for them also which shall believe on me through their word; 21 That they all may be one; as thou, Father, art in me, and I in thee, that they also may be one in us: that the world may believe that thou hast sent me. 22 And the glory which thou gavest me I have given them; that they may be one, even as we are one: 23 I in them, and thou in me, that they may be made perfect in one; and that the world may know that thou hast sent me, and hast loved them, as thou hast loved me. 24 Father, I will* *that they also, whom thou hast given me, be with me where I am; that they may behold my glory, which thou hast given me: for thou lovedst me before the foundation of the world. 25 O righteous Father, the world hath not known thee: but I have known thee, and these have known that thou hast sent me. 26 And I have declared unto them thy name, and will declare it: that the love wherewith thou hast loved me may be in them, and I in them.*

Stand tall with your head lifted high. You are His. **Romans 8:31-39 (KJV)** *31 What shall we then say to these things? If God be for us, who can be against us? 32 He that spared not his own Son, but delivered him up for us all, how shall he not with him also freely give us all things? 33 Who shall lay any thing to the charge of God's elect? It is God that justifieth. 34 Who is he that condemneth? It is Christ that died, yea rather, that is risen again, who is even at the right hand of God, who also maketh intercession for us. 35 Who shall separate us from the love of Christ? shall tribulation, or distress, or persecution, or famine, or nakedness, or peril, or sword? 36 As it is written, For thy sake we are killed all the day long; we are accounted as sheep for the slaughter. 37 Nay, in all these things we are more than conquerors through him that loved us. 38 For I am persuaded, that neither death, nor life, nor angels, nor principalities, nor powers, nor things present, nor things to come, 39 Nor height, nor depth, nor any other creature, shall be able to separate us from the love of God, which is in Christ Jesus our Lord.*

Sometimes when we look at our own weaknesses and failures, we forget who we are. But we are loved. We are saved. We are the ones that Jesus would not live without. We are set free, a purchased, ransomed, redeemed and regenerated people. There is no one else on earth any more important to God than we are. God has made us rich. God has washed us clean. We are His ambassadors and representatives. Believers have become the sent out, the commissioned of the Lord. We are endued with the very power of Christ and authorized to use His name.

Works Cited

Capps, Charles. Releasing the Ability of God: (Tulsa, OK: Harrison House, 1978) p. 10, 15, 34, 47, 92, 94, 152.

Capps, Charles. The Tongue a Creative Force: (Tulsa, OK: Harrison House, 1976) p. 7, 13, 90, 92.

Dollar, Creflo. The Image of Righteousness: You're More Than You Know: (Tulsa, OK: Harrison House, 2002) p. 7, 11, 17, 33, 60, 66.

Dufresne, Ed. There's a Healer in the House: (Temecula, CA: Ed Dufresne Ministries, 1993) p. 27.

Hagin, Kenneth. The Believer's Authority: (Tulsa, OK: Faith Library Publications, 1993) p. 7, 16, 17, 22, 27.

Henry, Matthew. Concise Commentary on the Whole Bible: (Chicago, IL: Moody, 1989).

Kenyon, E.W. The Wonderful Name of Jesus: (Lynnwood, WA: Kenyon's Gospel Publishing Society, 1964) p. 4, 5, 8, 22, 26, 39, 46, 48, 64.

Lindsey, Hal. Combat Faith: (Toronto, New York, London, Sydney, Auckland: Bantam Books, 1986) p. 21, 41, 75, 85, 86, 101, 104, 105, 184, 185.

Ortberg, John. If You Want to Walk on Water, You've Got to Get Out of the Boat: (Grand Rapids, MI: Zondervan Publishing House, 2001) p. 14, 17, 22, 23, 24, 118, 123.

Prince, Joseph. Daily Grace Inspirations. (Joseph Prince Ministries email devotional 9/28/17, 10/21/17, 10/23/17, 1/3/18)

Treat, Casey. Renewing the Mind: the Arena for Success: (Tulsa, OK: Harrison House, 1984) p. 22.

Trombley, Charles, Released to Reign: (Green Forest, AR: New Leaf Press. 1985) p. 19, 20, 27, 28, 62, 63, 70, 74, 85, 86, 101, 103, 104, 105, 106, 107, 109, 112, 117, 129,

130.

Author Page

I was saved in 1972, in a revival at Suburban Baptist Church in Granite City IL. I learned to love the Lord and His Word and began my walk there. In 1980, I was filled with the Holy Spirit at Full Gospel Evangelistic Center of Alton. It was there that I began to minister the Word in Power. God called me to "Build up the body of Christ," and I have been preaching and teaching all these years for that purpose. Becoming an author was a natural expansion of that call to minister. I love teaching and preaching and there is no greater joy than walking the path He places before me. I serve locally as an associate minister at The House of Victory in Cottage Hills IL, under Pastor Timothy Naylor. I am available for speaking engagements and would gladly come minister at your church or conference.

I Am Who God Says I Am is the fifth book that I have authored. If you were blessed by it, I would recommend that you read some of my others. There is Fire in the Blood, my first book, explores the blood sacrifices throughout time as they point to the Blood of Jesus and bring us the Fire of His presence. It was the same fire that fell on the sacrificial altars of Abel, Elijah, and Moses that produced the blaze of Pentecost. As we honor the blood and recognize its power we make way for the glory of God; if we want to experience the Fire, we know where to find it; 'There is Fire in the Blood.'

My second book, Meet Me on the Mountain, focuses on intimate fellowship with God. The mountain of God is that place where faith & hunger produce His presence. The drive to climb is not just man striving for God; it is an answer to the call. God loved us first and He is calling to the heart of man to draw nearer and stay longer in His presence. This book has more personal experiences included to demonstrate how He meets with us and longs for passionate fellowship with His children. If you seek Him—you will find Him.

My third book, <u>I Hear the Rocks Falling</u>, was inspired by the woman caught in adultery and thrown at the feet of Jesus. She expected the stones to crush her. Instead she heard the sound of the rocks falling to the ground as her accusers left. Like her, most of us have had moments of despair and shame and condemnation. Repeated offences deepen our sense of loss stacking one harsh, hardened, hurtful memory on top of another until we are bound within an internal prison. Jesus speaks to all of us to come out of those walls. We are to walk free from all condemnation and everything that has kept us tied to our past.

<u>Wilt Thou Be Made Whole</u> is an invitation to receive healing. On the cross, Jesus purchased salvation, and freedom from every consequence of Adam's fall. Healing belongs to us. It is not something we are trying to grasp; it was purchased for us by virtue of His broken body and shed blood. When we recognize that He bore our sickness like He bore our sin, we can access His healing power. Every word of testimony and scripture in this book was purposed to raise your faith so that you too can be free from sickness and disease. He is still asking, "Wilt Thou Be Made Whole?"

Contact information:
Fire in the Blood Ministries
Rev. Kathryn L. Smith
Email: klssaved1972@yahoo.com
Fire in the Blood Ministries also has a Facebook Page

KATHRYN L. SMITH

fbm/revkathy   or   m.me/revkathy

www.ingramcontent.com/pod-product-compliance
Lightning Source LLC
Chambersburg PA
CBHW071619080526
44588CB00010B/1195